Federal Financial Institutions Examination Council

ANNUAL REPORT 2009

30th ANNIVERSARY 1979 – 2009

Board of Governors of the Federal Reserve System, Federal Deposit Insurance Corporation, National Credit Union Administration, Office of the Comptroller of the Currency, Office of Thrift Supervision, State Liaison Committee

Federal Financial Institutions Examination Council

ANNUAL REPORT 2009

30th
ANNIVERSARY
1 9 7 9 – 2 0 0 9

Board of Governors of the Federal Reserve System, Federal Deposit Insurance Corporation, National Credit Union Administration, Office of the Comptroller of the Currency, Office of Thrift Supervision, State Liaison Committee

MEMBERS OF THE COUNCIL

Sheila C. Bair, *Chairman*
Chairman
Federal Deposit Insurance Corporation

John E. Bowman, *Vice Chairman*
Acting Director
Office of Thrift Supervision

Debbie Matz
Chairman
National Credit Union Administration

John C. Dugan
Comptroller of the Currency
Office of the Comptroller of the Currency

Daniel K. Tarullo
Member, Board of Governors of the
Federal Reserve System

John Munn
Director
Nebraska Department of Banking & Finance

LETTER OF TRANSMITTAL

Federal Financial Institutions
  Examination Council
Arlington, VA 22226
March 31, 2010

The President of the Senate
The Speaker of the House of Representatives

Pursuant to the provisions of section 1006(f) of the Financial Institutions Regulatory and Interest Rate Control Act of 1978 (12 U.S.C. § 3305), I am pleased to submit the 2009 Annual Report of the Federal Financial Institutions Examination Council.

Respectfully,

Sheila C Bair

Sheila C. Bair
Chairman

TABLE OF CONTENTS

Sheila C. Bair

The FFIEC, celebrating thirty years since its establishment by Congress, comprises the Board of Governors of the Federal Reserve System, the Federal Deposit Insurance Corporation, the Office of the Comptroller of the Currency, the National Credit Union Administration, and the Office of Thrift Supervision. In 2006, the State Liaison Committee was added to the Council as a voting member.

With a turbulent economy over the past few years and 140 bank failures in 2009, the FFIEC's role has become even more vital. The FFIEC has remained on the forefront of major policy initiatives by prescribing uniform principles, standards and report forms for the examination of financial institutions by state and federal banking, thrift, and credit union regulatory agencies.

Towards the overall goal of promoting uniformity in the supervision of financial institutions, I am pleased to report that the FFIEC continued its high level of performance and productivity throughout 2009.

Details on the 2009 achievements are included later in this report in the Record of Council Activities and Activities of the Interagency Staff Task Forces. I would like to recognize, however, some of the most significant initiatives that the Council, its task forces, and interagency working groups facilitated during the year:

- Issued for comment, in June 2009, proposed Interagency Guidance on Funding and Liquidity Management. The proposal summarizes the principles issued in previous guidance and brings them into conformance, where appropriate, with the Principles for Sound Liquidity Risk Management issued by the Basel Committee on Banking Supervision in September 2008.

- Issued for comment, in June 2009, proposed rules to implement the requirements of the Secure and Fair Enforcement for Mortgage Licensing Act of 2008.

- Issued, in July 2009, the Statement on Regulatory Conversions to reaffirm that the supervisors are unified in their approach to regulatory conversions.

- Issued, in August 2009, the statement on Support for Responsible Loss Mitigation Activities to reiterate support for responsible loss mitigation activities designed to preserve homeownership.

- Issued for comment, in September 2009, Correspondent Concentration Risks guidance on managing the credit and funding risks associated with large exposures to correspondent counterparties.

- Issued, in October 2009, a joint Policy Statement on Prudent Commercial Real Estate Loan Workouts. This statement is intended to promote supervisory consistency, enhance the transparency of CRE workout transactions, and ensure the supervisory policies and actions do not inadvertently curtail the availability of credit to sound borrowers.

- Approved for issuance, in December 2009, the Advisory on Interest Rate Risk, to remind institutions of supervisory expectations for sound risk management practices and to identify selected risk management techniques used by effective risk managers. The advisory was issued on January 6, 2010.

- Published final new and revised Community Reinvestment Act (CRA) Interagency Questions and Answers in January 2009 that, among other things, encouraged financial institutions to take steps to help prevent home mortgage foreclosures.

- Revised the Regulation DD (Truth in Savings) examination procedures to address depository institutions' disclosure practices related to the disclosures of aggregate overdraft and returned item fees on periodic statements and balance disclosures provided to consumers through automated systems.

- Developed interagency guidance on managing compliance and reputation risks for reverse mortgages. In December 2009, the agencies issued for public comment proposed Reverse Mortgage Products: Guidance for Managing Compliance and Reputation Risks.

- Finalized, in July 2009, a comprehensive set of questions and answers regarding flood insurance to help financial institutions meet their responsibilities under federal flood insurance legislation and to increase public understanding of the flood insurance regulations.

- Issued examination procedures for assessing compliance with the Servicemembers' Civil Relief Act (SCRA), which replaced the Soldiers' and Sailors' Civil Relief Act of 1940. The examination procedures reflect amendments to the SCRA that were enacted in 2004 and 2008.

- Updated Regulation Z examination procedures to incorporate regulatory and statutory changes as amended by the Home Ownership and Equity Protection Act, the Mortgage Disclosure Improvement Act of 2009, the Helping Families Save Their Homes Act of 2009, and the Credit Card Accountability

Responsibility and Disclosure Act of 2009.

- Revised the RESPA examination procedures to incorporate technical and substantive changes to the RESPA regulations issued by the Department of Housing and Urban Development.

- Revised the HMDA examination procedures to address changes to the requirements for reporting price information on higher-priced loans as a result of amendments to the HMDA regulations.

- Trained over 2,700 state and federal employees from various agencies through training sponsored by the FFIEC's Examiner Education Office.

- Offered a number of well-received training sessions for examiners, including a commercial real estate analysis course. Also, designed and piloted a new course on structured finance.

- Held a fraud investigations symposium. The symposium resulted in the creation of a white paper entitled, "The Detection and Deterrence of Mortgage Fraud Against Financial Institutions."

- Approved various reporting requirements for the Consolidated Reports of Condition and Income that addressed areas in which the banking industry had been experiencing heightened risk as a result of market turmoil and illiquidity, and weakening economic and credit conditions. Additional changes addressed recent developments including the temporary increase in the deposit insurance limit, changes in accounting standards, and credit availability concerns.

- Enhanced the Central Data Repository (CDR) for processing the quarterly bank Call Reports.

The reporting functionality for the Uniform Bank Performance Report within the CDR was implemented for agency use in December 2009.

- Enhanced the UBPR website to include, among others: income, expense, and loss data related to fiduciary activities; information about income or loss from minority interests; separate analysis of Other Real Estate Owned, Investments in Unconsolidated Subsidiaries, and Direct/Indirect Investments in Real Estate Ventures data; and, new information collected in the Call Report about Commercial Mortgage Backed Securities and Structured Financial Products.

- Completed the BASEL II XML implementation project. The agencies received the first production data in March 2009.

- Formed the Identity Management Working Group to explore sharing of information across agencies through a federated security architecture.

As evidenced by the foregoing initiatives, the FFIEC continues to do important work—thanks to the dedicated and talented full-time Council staff, as well as task force representatives from all the member agencies. Even though great progress was made throughout 2009, we have much more work to do in the coming year including the implementation of the SAFE Act in 2010.

Marking its thirtieth year since establishment, I believe the FFIEC, as Congress intended, continues to provide a valuable opportunity for the regulators to act—in a strong and unified voice and in a timely fashion—on supervisory policy issues that are relevant and of critical importance. I am, indeed, honored to serve as its Chairman.

OVERVIEW OF THE FEDERAL FINANCIAL INSTITUTIONS EXAMINATION COUNCIL (FFIEC) OPERATIONS

The FFIEC was established on March 10, 1979, pursuant to title X of the Financial Institutions Regulatory and Interest Rate Control Act of 1978 (FIRIRCA), Public Law 95-630. The purpose of title X, entitled the Federal Financial Institutions Examination Council Act of 1978, was to create a formal interagency body empowered to prescribe uniform principles, standards, and report forms for the federal examination of financial institutions by the Board of Governors of the Federal Reserve System, the Federal Deposit Insurance Corporation, the National Credit Union Administration, the Office of the Comptroller of the Currency, and the Office of Thrift Supervision and to make recommendations to promote uniformity in the supervision of financial institutions. In accordance with the Financial Services Regulatory Relief Act of 2006, a representative state regulator was added as a member of the FFIEC in October 2006. The Council is also responsible for developing uniform reporting systems for federally supervised financial institutions, their holding companies, and the nonfinancial institution subsidiaries of those institutions and holding companies. It conducts schools for examiners employed by the five federal member agencies represented on the Council and makes those schools available to employees of state agencies that supervise financial institutions.

The Council was given additional statutory responsibilities by section 340 of the Housing and Community Development Act of 1980, Public Law 96-399. Among these responsibilities are the implementation of a system to facilitate public access to data that depository institutions must disclose under the Home Mortgage Disclosure Act of 1975 (HMDA) and the aggregation of annual HMDA data, by census tract, for each metropolitan statistical area.

Title XI of the Financial Institutions Reform, Recovery, and Enforcement Act of 1989 established the Appraisal Subcommittee within the Council. The functions of the subcommittee are (1) monitoring the requirements, including a code of professional responsibility, established by states for the certification and licensing of individuals who are qualified to perform appraisals in connection with federally related transactions; (2) monitoring the appraisal standards established by the federal financial institution regulatory agencies and the former Resolution Trust Corporation; (3) maintaining a national registry of appraisers who are certified and licensed by a state and who are also eligible to perform appraisals in federally related transactions; and (4) monitoring the practices, procedures, activities, and organizational structure of the Appraisal Foundation, a nonprofit educational corporation established by the appraisal industry in the United States.

Title V of the Housing and Economic Recovery Act of 2008 established the responsibility for the federal banking agencies, through the FFIEC and in conjunction with the Farm Credit Administration, to develop and maintain a system for registering depository institution employees as registered loan originators with the Nationwide Mortgage Licensing System and Registry (NMLSR). The system shall, at a minimum, furnish or cause to be furnished to the NMLSR information concerning the employees' identity, including: (A) fingerprints for submission to the Federal Bureau of Investiga-

tion and any governmental agency or entity authorized to receive such information for a state and national criminal history background check; and (B) personal history and experience, including authorization for the NMLSR to obtain information related to any administrative, civil, or criminal findings by any governmental jurisdiction.

The Council has six members: a member of the Board of Governors of the Federal Reserve System appointed by the Chairman of the Board, the Chairman of the Federal Deposit Insurance Corporation, the Chairman of the Board of the National Credit Union Administration, the Comptroller of the Currency, the Director of the Office of Thrift Supervision, and the Chairman of the State Liaison Committee. To encourage the application of uniform examination principles and standards by the state and federal supervisory authorities, the Council established, in accordance with the requirement of the statute, an advisory State Liaison Committee. To effectively administer projects in all its functional areas, the Council established six interagency staff task forces, each of which includes one senior official from each of the member agencies:

- Consumer Compliance
- Examiner Education
- Information Sharing
- Reports
- Supervision
- Surveillance Systems

The Council also established the Legal Advisory Group, composed of the general or chief counsel of each of the member agencies, to provide support to the Council and staff in the substantive areas of concern;

and the Agency Liaison Group, composed of senior officials responsible for coordinating the efforts of their respective agencies' staff members. The task forces and the Legal Advisory Group provide research and analytical papers and proposals on the issues that the Council addresses.

Administration of the Council

The Council holds regular meetings at least twice a year. It holds other meetings whenever called by the Chairman or three or more Council members.

The Council's activities are funded in several ways. Most of the Council's funds are derived from assessments on its five federal member agencies. It receives tuition fees from non-agency attendees to cover some of the costs associated with its examiner education program. The Council also receives reimbursement for the services it provides to support preparation of the quarterly Uniform Bank Performance Report.

In 2009, the Federal Reserve Board provided budget and accounting services to the Council. The Council is supported by a small, full-time administrative staff in its operations office and in its examiner education program, which are located at the Council's examiner training facility in Arlington, Virginia. Each Council staff member is detailed from one of the five member agencies represented on the Council but is considered an employee of the Council.

The Federal Financial Institutions Examination Council in session.

The following section is a chronological record of the official actions taken by the FFIEC during 2009 pursuant to the Federal Financial Institutions Examination Council Act of 1978, as amended, and the Home Mortgage Disclosure Act (HMDA).

March 12, 2009

Action. Approved Memorandum of Understanding (MOU) by and between the FFIEC, Federal Deposit Insurance Corporation, Office of the Comptroller of the Currency, and Board of Governors of the Federal Reserve System regarding the duties and responsibilities for each production of the Uniform Bank Performance Report (UBPR) through 2011.

Explanation. The UBPR is an ongoing FFIEC project, however, the MOU that governs the production of the UBPR is signed for a three-year time frame to allow for periodic reviews and updates. The existing MOU expired at the end of 2008. Therefore, the MOU was updated and approved for three more years, until December 2011.

March 12, 2009

Action. Approved the appointment of six task force chairs.

Explanation. The chairs for all six standing task forces are approved annually and are drawn from management and staff of the five federal member agencies and representatives of the State Liaison Committee.

March 12, 2009

Action. Approved the 2008 annual report of the Council to the Congress.

Explanation. The legislation establishing the Council requires that, not later than April 1 of each year, the Council publish an annual

3

report covering its activities during the preceding year.

March 31, 2009

Action. Approved two new State Liaison Committee Members.

Explanation. The Council must approve two of the State Liaison Committee members—those who do not officially represent the Conference of State Banking Supervisors, the American Council of State Savings Supervisors, or the National Association of State Credit Union Supervisors.

March 31, 2009

Action. Approved the issuance of the Council's annual interagency awards.

Explanation. The Council has an interagency awards program that recognizes individuals of the member agencies who have provided outstanding service to the Council on interagency projects and programs during the previous year.

June 30, 2009

Action. Approved the issuance of the Council's Statement on Regulatory Conversions.

Explanation. The Council recognized the need to release a consistent joint statement to the industry to highlight the Council's commitment to assuring that there are no supervisory gaps associated with charter conversions.

August 12, 2009

Action. Approved Appraisal Subcommittee Chair.

Members of the Council engaged in discussions during the June 2009 Council meeting.

Explanation. The Council is required to approve the selection of the Appraisal Subcommittee Chair, who serves a two-year term.

October 13, 2009

Action. Approved funding for a second UBPR Coordinator.

Explanation. The Council is required to approve new positions. The second UBPR Coordinator will help to ensure continuity in the production of the UBPR.

December 1, 2009

Action. Approved the 2010 Council budget.

Explanation. The Council is required to approve the annual budget that funds the Council's staff, programs, and activities.

State Liaison Committee (from the left to right) Harold E. Feeney (TX), Charles A. Vice (KY), Douglas Foster (TX), Sarah Bloom Raskin (MD), and Chair John Munn (NE).

The Financial Services Regulatory Relief Act of 2006 made the Chairman of the State Liaison Committee a voting member of the council. With the passage of this act, the State Liaison Committee appointed state supervisors to represent the state system on all task forces and working groups. The State Liaison Committee's involvement with such groups enables state regulators to participate in substantive policy discussions on a broad range of important regulatory subjects, reflecting the spirit and intent of Congress in establishing the State Liaison Committee. The Conference of State Bank Supervisors serves as the primary liaison to the FFIEC for all administrative matters.

In response to their role on the Council, the State Liaison Committee meets in person before each Council meeting to review the agenda and discuss topics of interest which may come before the Council. This ensures the State Liaison Committee is fully versed on all issues before the Council.

In addition, to further state-federal supervisory efforts, the State Liaison Committee continues to encourage state regulatory authorities to adopt and implement those policies, guidelines, and examination procedures adopted by the Council.

The State Liaison Committee consists of five representatives of state regulatory agencies that supervise financial institutions. The representatives are appointed for two-year terms. A State Liaison Committee member may have his or her two-year term extended by the appointing organization for an additional, consecutive two-year term. Each year, the State Liaison Committee elects one of its members to serve as chair for twelve months. The Council elects two of the five members. The American Council of State Savings Supervisors, the Conference of State Bank Supervisors, and the National Association of State Credit Union Supervisors designate the other three members. A list of the State Liaison Committee members appears in Appendix D of this report.

ACTIVITIES OF THE INTERAGENCY STAFF TASK FORCES

Task Force on Consumer Compliance

The Task Force on Consumer Compliance promotes policy coordination, a common supervisory approach, and uniform enforcement of consumer protection laws and regulations. The task force identifies and analyzes emerging consumer compliance issues and develops proposed policies and procedures to foster consistency among the agencies. Additionally, the task force reviews legislation, regulations, and policies at the state and federal level that may have a bearing on the compliance responsibilities of the five federal member agencies.

During 2009, the task force used two standing subcommittees to help promote its mission: the Community Reinvestment Act (CRA) Subcommittee and the Home Mortgage Disclosure Act (HMDA)/CRA Data Collection Subcommittee. The

task force also creates ad hoc working groups to handle particular projects and assignments. The task force meets monthly to address and resolve common issues in compliance supervision. While significant issues or recommendations are referred to the FFIEC for action, the FFIEC has delegated to the task force the authority to make certain decisions and recommendations.

Initiatives Addressed in 2009

CRA Subcommittee Activities

The agencies published final new and revised CRA Interagency Questions and Answers in January 2009. Among other things, the agencies encouraged financial institutions to take steps to help prevent home mortgage foreclosures. In addition, the agencies published for comment one new and two revised questions and answers in response to comments received. Final action on

these proposed revisions is expected in early 2010.

HMDA/CRA Data Collection Subcommittee Activities

The HMDA and CRA Data Collection System re-architecture initiative is on schedule and on budget. Benefits associated with the HMDA 2010 re-architecture initiative relative to the current mainframe system include reduced data reporting and processing costs and enhanced agency access to updated HMDA and CRA data.

Beginning in 2010 the U.S. Census Bureau, as part of the American Community Survey, will begin reporting on our nation's population and housing for all geographies on an annual, three-year, and five-year basis. The task force is currently deciding how often to update the FFIEC Census file, given the availability of more frequent census data. More frequent updates will affect the geographic income levels used for CRA examinations, which, to-date, have only been updated every ten years.

Regulation DD (Truth in Savings)

The FFIEC agencies revised their Regulation DD (Truth in Savings) examination procedures to reflect requirements under the final rule amending Regulation DD to address depository institutions' disclosure practices related to the disclosures of aggregate overdraft and returned item fees on periodic statements and balance disclosures provided to consumers through automated systems.

Reverse Mortgages

The FFIEC agencies developed interagency guidance on managing compliance and reputation risks for reverse mortgages. On December 16, 2009, the agencies issued for public

Task Force on Consumer Compliance meeting.

7

comment proposed *Reverse Mortgage Products: Guidance for Managing Compliance and Reputation Risks.* The proposed guidance discusses the general features of, certain legal provisions applicable to, and consumer protection concerns raised by reverse mortgage products. In addition, the guidance focuses on the need to provide adequate information to consumers about reverse mortgage products; to provide qualified independent counseling to consumers considering these products; and to avoid potential conflicts of interest. The proposed guidance also addresses related policies, procedures, and internal controls and third-party risk management. Final action on the guidance is anticipated in mid-2010.

Consumer Complaints

The FFIEC agencies engaged in efforts to help consumers reach the appropriate regulator when seeking to resolve concerns with their financial institution. The agencies also continued to maintain and monitor the "Consumer Help Center," a consumer webpage launched in December 2008 to supplement the existing FFIEC website. The webpage assists consumers in identifying the appropriate regulator and provides links to the appropriate regulator's consumer complaint webpage. Consumers viewed the website 205,688 times in 2009. In addition, the working group meets regularly to share complaint data and discuss ways that the data might be used to identify emerging issues and aid in the development of consumer education materials.

Flood Insurance

In July 2009, the FFIEC agencies, along with the Farm Credit Administration, finalized a comprehensive set of questions and answers regarding flood insurance. This guidance includes both substantive and technical revisions to existing guidance to help financial institutions meet their responsibilities under federal flood insurance legislation and

to increase public understanding of the flood insurance regulations. The agencies proposed and solicited public comments on additional questions and answers regarding insurable value and force placement issues. Final action on these additional proposed questions and answers is expected in early 2010.

Servicemembers' Civil Relief Act (SCRA)

The FFIEC agencies issued examination procedures for assessing compliance with the SCRA, which replaced the Soldiers' and Sailors' Civil Relief Act of 1940. The examination procedures reflect amendments to the SCRA that were enacted in 2004 and 2008. Pursuant to the SCRA, military personnel who are on active deployment receive reduced interest rates on debts incurred before entering into military service. In addition, covered individuals receive protection from foreclosure or eviction during periods of military service and the nine months thereafter. The SCRA also prohibits lenders from repossessing vehicles purchased prior to active military service without a court order. Under the law, lenders may not take adverse action against a servicemember who invokes SCRA protection.

Regulation Z (Truth in Lending)

The FFIEC agencies updated Regulation Z examination procedures to incorporate regulatory and statutory changes as amended by the Home Ownership and Equity Protection Act, the Mortgage Disclosure Improvement Act of 2009, the Helping Families Save Their Homes Act of 2009, and the Credit Card Accountability Responsibility and Disclosure Act of 2009. The regulatory changes were intended to improve mortgage disclosures; prohibit unfair, abusive or deceptive mortgage lending and servicing practices; and address change-in-terms notice requirements and the amount of time that consumers have to make their credit card payments.

Real Estate Settlement Procedures Act (RESPA)

The FFIEC agencies revised their RESPA examination procedures to incorporate technical and substantive changes to the RESPA regulations issued by the Department of Housing and Urban Development. The centerpiece of these changes is the standardized Good Faith Estimate (GFE) form. As of January 1, 2010, a loan originator must provide a standard GFE form to a borrower within three business days of receipt of an application for a mortgage loan. With limited exceptions, the loan originator will be bound to the settlement charges and loan terms listed on the GFE. In addition, the regulations include a revised HUD-1/1A Settlement Statement form. To facilitate comparison between the HUD-1/1A and the GFE, each designated line on the HUD-1/1A includes a reference to the relevant line from the GFE.

Home Mortgage Disclosure Act (HMDA)

The FFIEC agencies revised their HMDA examination procedures to address changes to the requirements for reporting price information on higher-priced loans as a result of amendments to the HMDA regulations.

Task Force on Examiner Education

The Task Force on Examiner Education is responsible for overseeing the FFIEC's examiner education program on behalf of the Council. The task force promotes interagency education through timely, cost-efficient, state-of-the-art training programs for agency examiners and staff. The task force develops programs on its own initiative and in response to requests from the Council or other Council task forces. Each fall, task force staff prepares a training calendar based on demand from the five federal member agen-

Task Force on Examiner Education meeting.

Real Estate Analysis for Financial Institution Examiners course. This course has been added to the 2010 training calendar with 15 additional sessions. A Fraud Investigations Symposium was held in July 2009, creating a white paper entitled, "The Detection and Deterrence of Mortgage Fraud against Financial Institutions." This white paper substantially updates the February 2005 Mortgage Fraud white paper entitled, "The Detection, Investigation and Deterrence of Mortgage Loan Fraud Involving Third Parties." Both white papers are published on the FFIEC website, www.ffiec.gov. Additionally, a pilot session of a new course on Structured Finance was held and a second pilot will be held in 2010. Updates to the BSA/AML Examination Manual and the Information Technology Examination Handbook continue to be available to examiners and the industry through the FFIEC website.

cies and state financial institution regulators. Based on this demand, task force staff schedules, delivers, and evaluates training programs throughout the year. In 2009, over 2,700 people attended task force-sponsored training (see the table on the following page for details of participation by program and agency).

Initiatives Addressed in 2009

The Task Force on Examiner Education has continued to ensure that the FFIEC's educational programs meet the needs of agency personnel, are cost–effective, and are widely available. The task force meets monthly with the Examiner Education Office (EEO) staff to discuss emerging topics, to review feedback from each course and conference, and to develop a framework for future conferences and courses. The solid partnership between the task force principals and the EEO staff promotes open and regular commu-

nication that continues to result in high quality, well-received training.

Specific accomplishments during 2009 for the EEO were well received sessions of a Commercial

Facilities

FFIEC rents office space, classrooms, and lodging facilities at the Federal Deposit Insurance Corporation's Seidman Center in Arlington,

Stephen R. Gulbrandsen instructs at the FFIEC's Advanced Cash Flow Concepts & Analysis: Beyond the Numbers

Virginia. This facility offers convenient access to two auditoriums and numerous classrooms.

Course Catalogue and Schedule

The course catalogue and schedule are available online at www.ffiec. gov/exam/education.htm.

Additionally, a printed copy of the 2010 course catalogue and schedule are available from the EEO. To obtain a copy, contact:

Karen K. Smith, Manager
FFIEC Examiner Education Office
3501 Fairfax Drive
Room B-3030
Arlington, VA 22226-3550

Phone: (703) 516-5588

Task Force on Information Sharing

The Task Force on Information Sharing promotes the sharing of electronic information among FFIEC agencies in support of the supervision, regulation, and deposit insurance responsibilities of financial institution regulators. The task force provides a forum for FFIEC

2009 FFIEC Training by Agency and Sponsored—Actual, as of December 31, 2009

Event Name	FRB	FRB State Sponsored	FDIC	FDIC State Sponsored	NCUA	OCC	OTS	FCA	FHFB	Other	Total
Advanced BSA/AML Conference	25	12	35	27	13	17	16	0	0	12	157
Advanced Cash Flow Concepts & Analysis: Beyond	26	11	89	1	8	29	10	3	0	0	177
Advanced Commercial Credit Analysis	24	19	62	19	7	22	7	2	1	0	163
Anti-Money Laundering Workshop	18	17	28	26	15	0	23	0	0	12	139
Advanced Fraud Investigation Techniques for Examiners	12	9	8	0	5	6	1	0	0	0	41
Asset Management Forum	34	16	34	17	0	17	7	0	1	1	127
Capital Markets Conference	43	27	31	18	10	16	11	4	8	3	171
Capital Markets Specialists Conference	15	8	75	12	7	20	16	12	7	0	172
Cash Flow Construction and Analysis	30	22	84	36	21	28	15	1	0	1	238
Commercial Real Estate	10	0	24	0	3	53	9	0	0	0	99
Community Financial Institutions Lending Forum	17	7	73	14	10	13	8	3	1	0	146
Financial Crimes Seminar	53	30	48	11	27	0	33	0	1	9	212
Fraud Identification On-line Training	2	0	2	0	2	1	0	0	0	0	7
Fraud Investigations Symposium	4	0	5	0	2	3	2	0	0	1	17
FRB Fundamentals of Fraud	0	0	4	22	9	9	1	0	0	3	48
Information Technology Conference	41	12	22	3	17	35	36	11	5	0	182
Instructor Training School	25	1	0	0	4	4	0	2	0	1	37
International Banking School	9	5	4	2	0	5	0	0	0	0	25
International Banking (Self-Study)	10	0	6	0	1	6	0	0	0	5	28
Payment Systems Risk Conference	38	13	16	4	12	13	5	0	3	8	112
Real Estate Appraisal Review School	18	10	46	0	10	0	53	2	0	0	139
Real Estate Appraisal Review On-line	3	0	4	0	6	0	0	1	0	0	14
Structured Finance Pilot	5	0	5	0	4	5	3	0	0	3	25
Supervisory Updates & Emerging Issues	64	27	42	23	15	17	31	1	6	3	229
Testifying School	0	0	15	0	1	5	1	0	0	0	22
Grand Total	526	246	762	235	209	324	288	42	33	62	2,727
Percentage	19.29	9.02	27.94	8.62	7.66	11.88	10.56	1.54	1.21	2.27	100
Combined Agency and Sponsored Percentage	28.31	NA	36.56	NA	7.66	11.88	10.56	1.54	1.21	2.27	100

member agencies to discuss and address issues affecting the quality, consistency, efficiency, and security of interagency information sharing. Significant matters are referred, with recommendations, to the Council for action, and the task force has delegated authority from the Council to take certain actions.

To the extent possible, the agencies build on each other's information databases to minimize duplication of effort and promote consistency. The agencies participate in a program to share, in accordance with agency policy, electronic versions of their reports of examination, inspection reports, and other communications with financial institutions. The agencies also provide each other with access to their organizations' structure, financial, and supervisory information on their regulated entities. The task force and its working groups use a collaborative website to share information among the FFIEC agencies. The task force maintains a "Data Exchange Summary" listing the data files exchanged among FFIEC agencies and a repository of communications and documents critical to information sharing.

The task force has established one working group to address technology-development issues and another working group to perform interagency reconciliation of financial institution structure data. In addition, the task force receives demonstrations and reports on agency, financial industry, and other FFIEC initiatives pertaining to technology development, including the production and development status of the interagency Central Data Repository.

Initiatives Addressed in 2009

Technology Issues

The mission of the task force is to identify and implement technologies to make the sharing of interagency data more efficient and to accommodate changes in agency

Task Force on Information Sharing meeting.

databases and technologies. The task force's Technology Working Group (TWG) meets monthly to develop technological solutions to enhance data sharing and to coordinate the automated transfer of data files between the FFIEC agencies. Due to the ongoing NIC Architecture Redesign Initiative (NARI), the group is currently tracking all progress via the Interagency Data Exchange (IADE) Project Plan. The group is heavily involved with the interagency transition to XML, delta files, and Connect: Direct.

The TWG continues to develop necessary links and processes to exchange electronic documents; develop an inventory of future technology projects; and upload information to the collaborative website where documents and critical materials pertaining to interagency information exchanges are stored. TWG efforts addressed in 2009 include:

- *BASEL II*—Agencies completed a final "end-to-end" test in February and upon successful results, FRB migrated BASEL II XML generation and transfer systems to production. Agencies received the first production data on March 4, 2009. Therefore the BASEL II implementation project is complete.

- *SNC Modernization*—FRB distributed XML schemas to the agencies. XML test data also has been distributed to the agencies.

- *Interagency Data Exchange (IADE) Project Plan Update*—Agencies neared completion of the effort to migrate data series from mainframe BulkData transfer to Connect:Direct / XML processes. Only one series (SURV) from FRB to FDIC remains on BulkData. The conversion of SURV will be complete by January 29, 2010, completing the BulkData conversion effort.

Supervisory information (EVE data) from OCC to FDIC has been converted to XML feeds from a twice-a-month transfer of data on DVD. OCC now sends EVE data to all receiving agencies via XML.

Structure Data Reconciliation

The task force's Structure Data Reconciliation Working Group (SDRWG) continued to reconcile structure data about financial institutions regulated by FFIEC agencies to ensure that the information the agencies report is consistent and accurate. The SDRWG's quarterly reconcilements have greatly resolved data discrepancies among the agencies.

Identity Management

In 2009, the task force agreed to explore a Proof of Concept in sharing of information across agencies through federated security architecture. To do so, the Identity Management Working Group was formed with participation from each agency and a project charter created. The group developed a presentation describing the current inefficiencies that exist today with isolated security. The work group is in the investigative phase of analyzing the issues to prepare the business case for moving forward. Progress on this effort will need to align with the direction from the individual agencies' Information Security Offices. A workshop is slated for late January to discuss the concept of 'federated security' and to begin the development of an MOU.

Task Force on Reports

The law establishing the Council and defining its functions requires the Council to develop uniform reporting systems for federally supervised financial institutions and their holding companies and subsidiaries. To meet this objective, the Council established the Task Force on Reports. The task force helps to develop interagency uniformity in the reporting of periodic information that is needed for effective supervision and other public policy purposes. As a consequence, the task force is concerned with issues such as the development and interpretation of reporting instructions, including responding to inquiries about the instructions from reporting institutions and the public; the application of accounting standards to specific transactions; the development and application of processing standards; the monitoring of data quality; and the assessment of reporting burden. In addition, the task force works with other organizations, including the Securities and Exchange Commission, the Financial Accounting Standards Board, and the American Institute of Certified Public Accountants. The task force is also responsible for any special projects related to these subjects that the Council may assign.

To help the task force carry out its responsibilities, working groups are organized as needed to handle specialized or technical accounting, reporting, instructional, and processing matters. In this regard, the task force has established a Central Data Repository (CDR) Steering Committee to make business decisions needed to ensure the success of the CDR initiative, monitor the project status, and report on its progress. The CDR is a secure shared database for collecting, managing, validating, and distributing data reported in the quarterly Consolidated Reports of Condition and Income (Call Report) filed by insured commercial banks and state-chartered savings banks.

Initiatives Addressed in 2009

Reporting Requirements for the Consolidated Reports of Condition and Income

In January 2009, the task force approved a final Paperwork Reduction Act (PRA) *Federal Register* notice on revisions to the Call Report that had been issued for public comment in September 2008. The revisions incorporated limited modifications made in response to comments received on the proposed changes. The reporting changes included new data items addressing areas in which the banking industry had been experiencing heightened risk as a result of market turmoil and illiquidity and weakening economic and credit conditions. The Federal Deposit Insurance Corporation (FDIC), the Federal Reserve Board, and the Office of the Comptroller of the Currency (collectively, the banking agencies) published the final PRA notice on the revised reporting requirements in January 2009. The U.S. Office of Management and Budget (OMB) approved these revisions in March 2009. The

Task Force on Report's Central Data Repository (CDR) Steering Committee meeting.

reporting changes were implemented in three phases:

- A limited group of Call Report revisions took effect on March 31, 2009. These revisions responded to new accounting standards, exempted banks with less than $1 billion in total assets from reporting certain existing Call Report items, clarified the definition of the term "loan secured by real estate," provided instructional guidance on quantifying misstatements in the Call Report, and eliminated confidential treatment for data collected from trust institutions on fiduciary income, expenses, and losses.

- The Call Report revisions made as of June 30, 2009, some of which apply only to banks meeting specified reporting thresholds, included new or revised items for real estate construction and development loans with interest reserves, holdings of commercial mortgage-backed securities and structured financial products, recurring fair value measurements for certain assets and liabilities, pledged loans and pledged trading assets, collateral and counterparties associated with over-the-counter derivative exposures, credit derivatives, remaining maturities of unsecured other borrowings and subordinated debt, and unused short-term commitments to asset-backed commercial paper conduits.

- The Call Report revisions that took effect December 31, 2009, apply only to trust institutions that complete Schedule RC-T, Fiduciary and Related Services. The revisions involved the types of fiduciary accounts for which fiduciary assets and income are reported, the types of assets and fiduciary accounts for which managed assets are reported, and data on debt issues in default under corporate trusteeships. The Office of Thrift Supervision (OTS) separately made comparable revisions to the Fiduciary and Related

Services schedule in the Thrift Financial Report (TFR) for savings associations.

During the second quarter, the task force evaluated recommendations from the banking agencies for potential Call Report revisions to be implemented in 2010. After considering the purposes for which the proposed additional data would be used, as well as the estimated cost and burden to banks of reporting these data, the task force approved, and the banking agencies published, an initial PRA *Federal Register* notice requesting comment on the proposed Call Report revisions in August 2009. The proposed revisions responded to such recent developments as a temporary increase in the deposit insurance limit, changes in accounting standards, and credit availability concerns. The proposed reporting changes for March 31, 2010, included new data on other-than-temporary impairments of debt securities, loans to nondepository financial institutions, and brokered time deposits; additional data on certain time deposits and unused commitments; and a change from annual to quarterly reporting for small business and small farm lending data and for the number of certain deposit accounts. The banking agencies also proposed to collect new data pertaining to reverse mortgages annually beginning December 31, 2010. The OTS incorporated several of the proposed Call Report revisions into a separate proposal for the TFR. After modifying the proposed Call Report changes in response to the comments received, the task force approved a final PRA *Federal Register* notice, which the banking agencies published in December 2009. OMB must approve these changes before they become final.

In November 2009, the task force initiated a project to combine the two Call Report forms into one form. A single form would reduce redundancies when the banking agencies implement metadata changes in the CDR system whenever the

Call Report forms or instructions are revised. Combining the two Call Report forms into a single form is not intended to increase the amount of data that any bank is currently required to report each quarter. Implementation of this change would be subject to notice and comment and would not take effect before March 2011.

The task force conducted monthly interagency conference calls during 2009 to discuss Call Report instructional matters and related accounting issues to reach uniform interagency positions on these issues.

Central Data Repository

During 2009, the agencies continued to devote significant staff resources to enhancing the CDR for processing the quarterly bank Call Reports.

A number of modifications were made to the Call Report processing and the public data distribution functionality. The majority of the work during 2009 centered on the tasks associated with the development of the Uniform Bank Performance Report (UBPR) within the CDR. Several releases occurred during 2009 to implement the UBPR functionality and prepare for report distribution to the public. In June 2009 the core functionality for financial ratio management and calculation was implemented. The reporting functionality was implemented for agency use in December 2009. Given the complexity of the UBPR information and a desire for additional testing, the banking agencies agreed to require another quarter of testing to validate the reporting results with the current UBPR system prior to making the information ready for publication as the system of record. The CDR Steering Committee is working in conjunction with the Task Force on Surveillance Systems to fully implement the UBPR within the CDR in 2010.

Other Activities

In March 2009, the task force

approved a final PRA *Federal Register* notice for the addition of two data items to the Call Report, the TFR, and the Report of Assets and Liabilities of U.S. Branches and Agencies of Foreign Banks (FFIEC 002 report) to support the FDIC's assessment calculations for institutions participating in its Transaction Account Guarantee Program (TAGP). The agencies' final PRA notice also included a new data item for the Call Report and the TFR on reciprocal brokered deposits needed for FDIC deposit insurance assessment purposes beginning in June 2009. In November 2008 OMB had granted emergency approval to the banking agencies and the OTS (collectively, the agencies) for the collection of the two TAGP data items through May 2009. The agencies were then required to follow OMB's normal clearance procedures to obtain approval to collect these items in the three reports each quarter until the end of the TAGP. These procedures included the agencies' publication of an initial PRA notice for these items in December 2008. The agencies' final PRA *Federal Register* notice was published in April 2009 and OMB approved the changes to the three reports in June 2009.

OMB approved three-year extensions of the authority for the banking agencies to collect the Country Exposure Reports (FFIEC 009 and 009a) and the Country Exposure Report for U.S. Branches and Agencies of Foreign Banks (FFIEC 019) in March and September 2009, respectively. OMB also approved a three-year extension of the banking agencies' authority to collect the Foreign Branch Report of Condition (FFIEC 030 and 030S) in November 2009. These approvals followed the banking agencies' publication of initial and final PRA *Federal Register* notices.

Task Force on Supervision

The Task Force on Supervision coordinates and oversees matters relating to safety-and-soundness supervision and examination of depository institutions. It provides a forum for the member agencies and State Liaison Committee to promote quality, consistency, and effectiveness in examination and supervisory practices. While significant issues are referred, with recommendations, to the Council for action, the Council has delegated to the task force the authority to make certain decisions and recommendations, provided all task force members agree. Meetings are held regularly to address and resolve common supervisory issues. The task force has also established and maintains supervisory communication protocols to be used in emergencies. These protocols are periodically tested through table-top exercises with task force members and key supervisory personnel.

The task force has two subcommittees and a standing working group:

- The *Capital Subcommittee* serves as a forum for senior policy staff members to discuss various initiatives pertaining to the agencies' regulatory capital standards.

- The *Information Technology (IT) Subcommittee* serves as a forum to address information systems and technology policy issues as they relate to financial institutions. The IT Subcommittee oversees and administers the FFIEC member agencies' Technology Service Provider (TSP) Examination and Shared Application Software Review (SASR) programs. Through the FFIEC'S Multi-Regional Data Processing Servicer program, the agencies conduct joint information technology examinations of the largest, systemically important technology service providers and other entities that provide critical banking services. The SASR program provides a mechanism for the agencies to review and share information on mission-critical software applications, such as loans, deposits, general ledger systems, and other critical software tools that are used by a large number of financial institutions. These programs help the agencies identify potential systemic risks and provide examiners with information that can reduce time and resources needed to examine the IT-related processing software and external services at user financial institutions.

- The *Bank Secrecy Act/Anti-Money Laundering (BSA/AML) Working Group* seeks to enhance coordination of BSA/AML training, guidance, and policy. The coordination includes continuing communication between federal and state banking agencies and the Financial Crimes Enforcement Network. The BSA/AML Working Group builds on existing efforts and works to strengthen the activities that are already being pursued by other formal and informal interagency groups providing oversight of various BSA/AML matters. BSA/AML training, guidance, and policy includes: (1) procedures and resource materials for examination purposes; (2) joint examiner training related to the FFIEC's BSA/AML Examination Manual; (3) outreach to the banking industry on BSA/AML policy matters; and (4) other issues related to consistency of BSA/AML supervision.

The task force also establishes ad hoc working groups to handle individual projects and assignments, as needed.

Initiatives Addressed in 2009

Statement on Regulatory Conversions

The Task Force on Supervision, at the direction of the FFIEC, developed the Statement on Regulatory Conversions (Statement). The Statement, issued July 2009, reaffirmed that the federal banking supervisors are unified in their approach to regulatory conversions in that the supervisors will only consider applications undertaken for legitimate reasons and will not entertain regulatory conversion applications

Task Force on Supervision meeting.

that undermine the supervisory process. It is expected prospective supervisors will follow existing supervisors' work on examination and enforcement actions, including consumer protection and safety and soundness issues.

SAFE Act

A task force working group, together with the Farm Credit Administration (FCA), continued to coordinate efforts among the FFIEC agencies to implement provisions of the Secure and Fair Enforcement for Mortgage Licensing Act of 2008 (the Act). As required by the Act, mortgage loan originators (MLOs) employed by institutions that are regulated by a federal banking agency or the FCA must register with the Nationwide Mortgage Licensing System and Registry (NMLSR), obtain a unique identifier and maintain this registration. As envisioned, the NMLSR will improve the flow of information to and between regulators, providing increased accountability and tracking of MLOs, enhancing consumer protections, and providing consumer access to certain information on MLOs. In June 2009, the FFIEC agencies and the FCA issued for public comment proposed rules to implement the requirements of the SAFE Act. The FDIC's Board of Directors approved the draft final rule implementing the SAFE Act on November 12, 2009. (A final regulation is to be issued in early 2010.)

Commercial Real Estate (CRE) Lending

Throughout the economic turmoil, FFIEC members have encouraged financial institutions to work constructively with borrowers who may be facing financial difficulty and to extend credit in a responsible and prudent manner. In 2009, in light of the sharp deterioration in the credit performance of CRE loans held in the portfolios of banks and thrifts, and those backing commercial mortgage-backed securities, the task force formed a working group to update previously issued supervisory issuances on the topic. This effort culminated in the FFIEC member agencies each issuing, on October 30, 2009, a joint *Policy Statement on Prudent Commercial Real Estate Loan Workouts*. This statement is intended to promote supervisory consistency, enhance the transparency of CRE workout transactions, and ensure the supervisory policies and actions do not inadvertently curtail the availability of credit to sound borrowers.

Enhanced Risk Management Practices

Current financial market and economic conditions present significant risk management challenges to institutions of all sizes. In this challenging environment, the task force established working groups to prepare the following issuances, which serve to reaffirm supervisory expectations for sound risk management practices by federal financial institutions:

- On June 30, 2009, the FFIEC member agencies, in conjunction with Conference of State Bank Supervisors (CSBS), issued for public comment proposed Interagency Guidance on Funding and Liquidity Management. The proposal summarized the principles issued in previous guidance, and brought them in conformity with the Principles for Sound Liquidity Risk Management issued by the Basel Committee on Banking Supervision in September 2008.

- In light of historically low short-term interest rates, it is important for institutions to have robust processes for measuring, and where necessary, mitigating their exposure to interest rate risk. The task force prepared an advisory on the topic to remind institutions of supervisory expectations for sound risk management practices and to identify selected risk management techniques used by effective risk managers. (On January 6, 2010, the Advisory on Interest Rate Risk was issued jointly by the FFIEC member agencies and CSBS.)

- On September 25, 2009, the OCC, OTS, FRB, and FDIC sought to address the concentration risk attendant to correspondent banking relationships by issuing for comment guidance on managing the credit and funding risk associated with large exposures to correspondent counterparties.

- To reiterate support for responsible loss mitigation activities designed to preserve homeownership, the task force prepared a statement that was issued by the FFIEC members on August 6, 2009. This support extends to programs designed to achieve sustainable mortgage obligations regardless of lien position.

Information Technology

Financial institutions' significant use of information technology services, whether generated internally or obtained from third-party service providers, contributes to their operational risk environment in general and their data security risk in particular. A major effort of the Information Technology Subcommittee (Subcommittee) and agencies is maintaining the FFIEC Information Technology handbook, which was first published in 1996. The handbook now consists of a series of topical booklets addressing issues such as business continuity planning, information security, and electronic banking.

The Subcommittee, in conjunction with the Task Force on Examiner Education, sponsors an annual Information Technology conference for the agencies' examination staff on emerging risks and industry best practices. The Subcommittee is also responsible for the coordination of the Multiregional Data Processing Servicer (MDPS) Program Oversight, which is ongoing. The FFIEC member agencies examine MDPS organizations because these entities pose a systemic risk to the banking system should one or more have operational or financial problems or fail. Since these companies service banks, thrifts, and credit unions, the FFIEC member agencies conduct interagency examinations of these large technology service providers. Interagency examinations provide a single examination report for the service providers. In March 2009 the Subcommittee held a supervisory strategy meeting with interagency examination teams from each MDPS to approve the examination strategies and schedules.

During the year, the Subcommittee devoted resources to enhancing the FFIEC member agencies' assessments of the financial condition of technology service providers. The Subcommittee also completed updates to the FFIEC member agencies' Shared Application Software Review (SASR) Program. The task force approved the original SASR program in 1990 to provide a uniform report on widely used software applications to the agencies and non-information technology examiners who examine banks using these software applications. The purpose of the program remains the same; however, the uniform report was revised in 2009 to enhance the efficiency of the review process and its use as a tool for safety and soundness examiners when assessing deficiencies in an institution's information technology function.

Capital Standards

Although each of the four federal banking agencies has its own capital regulations, the task force's standing Capital Subcommittee and several of its working groups promote joint issuance of capital rules and related interpretive guidance, thereby minimizing interagency differences and reducing the potential burden on the banking industry. The federal banking agencies have been re-examining our capital adequacy framework in light of the recent financial stress.

BSA/AML Working Group

The BSA/AML working group sponsored its third FFIEC BSA/AML Advanced Specialists Conference in August 2009. Feedback from the conference was positive. The BSA/AML working group completed the drafting of the BSA/AML examination manual in 2009 for publication in 2010. The revision will clarify supervisory expectations and incorporate regulatory changes since the manual's first release in 2005. The agencies continued to share information with the Financial Crimes Enforcement Network and with the Office of Foreign Assets Control.

Task Force on Surveillance Systems

The Task Force on Surveillance Systems oversees the development and implementation of uniform interagency surveillance and monitoring systems. It provides a forum for the member agencies to discuss best practices to be used in those systems and to consider the development of new financial analysis tools. The task force's principal objective has been to develop and produce the Uniform Bank Performance Report (UBPR). UBPRs present financial statistics and peer group comparisons of individual banks for current and historical periods. These reports are important tools for completing supervisory evaluations of a bank's condition and performance, as well as for planning onsite examinations. The banking agencies also use the data from these reports in their automated monitoring systems to identify potential or emerging problems in insured banks.

A UBPR is produced for each commercial bank and insured savings bank in the United States that is supervised by the Federal Reserve Board, the Federal Deposit Insurance Corporation, or the Office of the Comptroller of the Currency. UBPR data are also available to all state bank supervisors. While the UBPR is principally designed to meet the examination and surveillance needs of the federal and state banking agencies, the task force also makes the UBPR available to banks and the public through a public website, www.ffiec.gov.

Initiatives Addressed in 2009

Fiduciary Data Enhanced

The task force enhanced the UBPR website to allow income, expense, and loss data related to fiduciary activities to be displayed from March 31, 2009 forward. This change will broaden public access to information about fiduciary activities engaged in by banks and is consistent with a change to reporting standards for the Call Report. Additionally several ratios within the fiduciary section of the UBPR were updated to take advantage of new Call Report data that banks began reporting with the December 31, 2009 Call Report.

Task Force on Surveillance Systems meeting.

UBPR Available For Non-Insured Trust Companies

The task force took steps to allow UBPR reports to be delivered for approximately 90 Non Insured Trust Companies. Those trust companies file Call Reports and the creation of a new peer group number 401 will allow a UBPR to be produced for each of those banks. The change was made retroactively and will provide a financial analysis of this group of special purpose banks.

Minority Interest in Consolidated Subsidiaries Data Expanded

The task force expanded the UBPR income statement to include information about income or loss from minority interests. Additionally, ratios and related peer group statistics were added to the summary ratios section. The balance sheet treatment of capital was revised to include Minority Interests in Consolidated Subsidiaries. These changes were made retroactively.

Other Real Estate Owned, Investments in Unconsolidated Subsidiaries and Direct/Indirect Investments in Real Estate Ventures Data Expanded

The task force expanded the balance sheet presentation in the UBPR to include separate analysis of Other Real Estate Owned, Investments in Unconsolidated Subsidiaries and Direct/Indirect Investments in Real Estate Ventures data. These changes were made to the UBPR pages that display the balance sheet in both dollar and percentage format. The changes were retroactive and include peer group statistics where appropriate. This new data should provide analysts with more insight into the level of bank involvement in these activities.

Investment Portfolio Analysis Expanded

The task force expanded the investment portfolio analysis within the UBPR to include new information collected in the Call Report about Commercial Mortgage Backed Securities and Structured Financial Products. Captions for both of those categories were added to both the 'available for sale' and 'held to maturity' sections of the investment portfolio analysis. In addition to ratios, peer group statistics were added from June 30, 2009 forward. Several existing ratios within the investment portfolio analysis were updated to reflect changed defini-

tions. This new information should provide more information about the investment activities of commercial banks.

UBPR Delivered to a Wide Audience

UBPR for December 31, 2008; March 31, 2009; June 30, 2009; and September 30, 2009 was produced and delivered during 2009 to federal and state banking agencies. Additionally, the UBPR website was utilized to deliver the same data to bankers and the general public. The task force strives to deliver the most up-to-date UBPR data to all users. Thus current and historic UBPR data is updated at a minimum of once a week and more frequently during the time when new Call Report data is being submitted by banks.

Enhancements Planned to the UBPR

In 2010 the task force plans several enhancements to the UBPR that will take advantage of new and existing Call Report data. Included in those changes will be information about the volume of and rates paid on brokered deposits. Additionally the task force will review the current presentation of deposits and fiduciary activities in the UBPR and consider possible improvements to that information. The task force will continue to work closely with the Task Force on Reports and the Central Data Repository (CDR) Steering Committee in implementing a move of UBPR processing to the CDR.

Information Available on the UBPR Website

UBPR Availability

To provide broad public access to information about the financial condition of insured banks, the task force publishes a final quarterly version of the UBPR for each institution, typically within fifteen to twenty days of the Call Report due date. Additionally, early UBPR data is typically available fifteen days before the Call Report filing date. Bankers and the general public may access these reports on the FFIEC website at no charge. In addition to publishing current reports, the task force regularly refreshes all historic UBPR data on the website.

Other UBPR Reports

Several web-based statistical reports supporting UBPR analysis are also updated on the website. These reports (1) summarize the performance of each of the UBPR's peer groups (determined by size, location, and business line), (2) detail the distribution of UBPR performance ratios for banks in each of these peer groups, (3) list the individual banks included in each peer group, and (4) compare a bank to the performance of a user-defined custom peer group.

Custom Peer Group Tool

The Custom Peer Group Tool allows bankers, bank supervisors, and the general public to create custom peer groups based on financial and geographical criteria and to display all UBPR pages with peer group statistics and percentile rankings derived from a custom peer group.

Please visit www.ffiec.gov/UBPR. htm for additional information

about the UBPR, including distribution schedules, descriptions of pending changes, and instructions on using online UBPR tools. Standardized UBPR quarterly data in delimited files on DVD is also available for $400. Information on ordering items may be obtained by calling (703) 516-1071, sending an e-mail message to FFIEC_UBPR@ fdic.gov, or writing the Council at:

Federal Financial Institutions
    Examination Council
3501 Fairfax Drive, Room D8073a
Arlington, VA 22226-3550

The five federal financial institution regulatory agencies represented on the Council have primary federal supervisory jurisdiction over 15,789 domestically chartered banks, thrift institutions, and credit unions. On December 31, 2009, these financial institutions held total assets of more than $15.8 trillion. The Board of Governors of the Federal Reserve System and the Office of Thrift Supervision also have primary federal supervisory responsibility for commercial bank holding companies and for savings and loan holding companies, respectively.

Three banking agencies on the Council have authority to oversee the operations of U.S. branches and agencies of foreign banks. The International Banking Act of 1978 (IBA) authorizes the Office of the Comptroller of the Currency to license federal branches and agencies of foreign banks and permits U.S. branches that accept only wholesale deposits to apply for insurance with the Federal Deposit Insurance Corporation. According to the Federal Deposit Insurance Corporation Improvement Act of 1991 (FDICIA), foreign banks that wish to operate insured entities in the United States and accept retail deposits must organize under separate U.S. charters. Existing insured retail branches may continue to operate as branches. The IBA also subjects those U.S. offices of foreign banks to many provisions of the Federal Reserve Act and the Bank Holding Company Act. The IBA gives primary examining authority to the Office of the Comptroller of the Currency, the Federal Deposit Insurance Corporation, and various state authorities for the offices within their jurisdictions and gives the Federal Reserve Board residual examining authority over all U.S. banking operations of foreign banks.

Board of Governors of the Federal Reserve System

The Federal Reserve Board was established in 1913. It is headed by a seven-member Board of Governors, each member of which is appointed by the President, with the advice and consent of the Senate, for a fourteen-year term. Subject to confirmation by the Senate, the President selects two Board members to serve four-year terms as Chairman and Vice Chairman. The Federal Reserve Board's activities that are most relevant to the work of the Council are the following:

- examining, supervising, and regulating state member banks (that is, state-chartered banks that are members of the Federal Reserve System); bank holding companies; Edge Act and agreement corporations; and, in conjunction with the licensing authorities, the U.S. offices of foreign banks;

- developing and issuing regulations, policies, and guidance applicable to organizations within the Federal Reserve Board's supervisory oversight authority; and

- approving or denying applications for mergers, acquisitions, and changes in control by state member banks and bank holding companies; applications for foreign operations of member banks and Edge Act and agreement corporations; and applications by foreign banks to establish or acquire U.S. banks and to establish U.S. branches, agencies, or representative offices.

Other supervisory and regulatory responsibilities of the Federal Reserve Board include regulating margin requirements on securities transactions, implementing certain statutes that protect consumers in credit and deposit transactions, monitoring compliance with other statutes (for example, the money-laundering provisions of the Bank Secrecy Act), and regulating transactions between banking affiliates.

Policy decisions are implemented by the Federal Reserve Board and the twelve Federal Reserve Banks, each of which has operational responsibility within a specific geographical area. The twelve Reserve Bank Districts are headquartered in Boston, New York, Philadelphia, Cleveland, Richmond, Atlanta, Chicago, St. Louis, Minneapolis, Kansas City, Dallas, and San Francisco. Each Reserve Bank has a president and other officers. Among other responsibilities, a Reserve Bank employs a staff of bank examiners who examine state member banks and Edge Act and agreement corporations, inspect bank holding companies,

and examine the offices of foreign banks located within the Reserve Bank's District.

National banks, which must be members of the Federal Reserve, are chartered, regulated, and supervised by the Office of the Comptroller of the Currency. State-chartered banks may apply to and be accepted for membership in the Federal Reserve System, after which they are subject to the supervision and regulation of the Federal Reserve Board. Insured state-chartered banks that are not members of the

Federal Reserve System are regulated and supervised by the Federal Deposit Insurance Corporation. The Federal Reserve Board has overall responsibility for foreign banking operations, including both U.S. banks operating abroad and foreign banks operating branches in the United States.

The Federal Reserve Board covers the expenses of its operations with revenue it generates principally from assessments on the twelve Federal Reserve Banks.

Federal Deposit Insurance Corporation

Congress created the Federal Deposit Insurance Corporation (FDIC) in 1933 with a mission to insure bank deposits and reduce the economic disruptions caused by bank failures. Management of the FDIC is vested in a five-member Board of Directors. Three of the directors are directly appointed by the President, with the advice and consent of the Senate, for six-year terms. One of the three directors is designated by the President as Chairman for a term of five years, and another is designated as Vice Chairman. The other two Board members are the Comptroller of the Currency and the Director of the Office of Thrift Supervision. No more than three board members may be of the same political party.

The FDIC's supervisory activities are conducted by the Division of Supervision and Consumer Protection. The division is organized into six regional offices and two area offices. The regional offices are located in Atlanta, Chicago, Dallas, Kansas City, New York, and San Francisco. The two area offices are located in Boston (reports to New York) and Memphis (reports to Dallas). In addition to the regional and area offices, the FDIC maintains fifty-two field territory offices for risk management and thirty-two field territory offices for compliance, with dedicated

examiners assigned to the four largest financial institutions. Bank liquidations are handled by the Division of Resolutions and Receiverships.

The FDIC insures deposits at all insured commercial banks and savings institutions. On October 3, 2008, the Emergency Economic Stabilization Act of 2008 was approved, temporarily raising the standard maximum deposit insurance amount (SMDIA) on federal deposit insurance coverage from $100,000 to $250,000 per depositor through December 31, 2009. On May 20, 2009, the Helping Families Save Their Homes Act was approved, extending the SMDIA temporary increase to $250,000 per depositor through December 31, 2013. The legislation provides that the SMDIA will return to $100,000 on January 1, 2014, except for certain retirement accounts, which were permanently increased to $250,000 in 2006.

On September 9, 2009, the FDIC Board of Directors approved a rule to finalize the deposit insurance coverage regulations to reflect the extension of the temporary increase in the SMDIA to $250,000 through December 31, 2013. The Board also approved final rules for both the 2008 interim rules regarding revocable trust accounts (with some minor changes) and final rules for calculating coverage for mortgage servicing accounts.

In 2008, the FDIC's Board of Directors approved temporary deposit insurance changes under the Temporary Liquidity Guarantee Program (TLGP). The TLGP consists of two basic components: a guarantee of newly issued senior unsecured debt of banks, thrifts, and certain holding companies (known as the debt guarantee program) and full guarantee of noninterest-bearing deposit transaction accounts, such as business payroll accounts, regardless of dollar amount (known as the transaction account guarantee program or TAGP). On August 26, 2009, the FDIC adopted the final rule extending the TAGP portion of the TLGP for six months, through June 30, 2010.

Any depository institution that receives deposits may be insured by the FDIC after application to and examination and approval by the FDIC. After considering the (1) applicant's financial history

and condition, (2) adequacy of the capital structure, (3) future earnings prospects, (4) general character of the management, (5) risk presented to the insurance fund, (6) convenience and needs of the community to be served, and (7) consistency of corporate powers, the FDIC may approve or deny an application for insurance. The Federal Deposit Insurance Corporation Improvement Act of 1991 (FDICIA) expanded the FDIC's approval authority to include national banks, all state-chartered banks that are members of the Federal Reserve System, and federal and state-chartered savings associations.

The FDIC has primary federal regulatory and supervisory authority over insured state-chartered banks that are not members of the Federal Reserve System, and it has the authority to examine for insurance purposes any insured financial institution, either directly or in cooperation with state or other federal supervisory authorities. The FDICIA gives the FDIC backup enforcement authority over all insured institutions; that is, the FDIC can recommend that the appropriate federal agency take action against an insured institution and may do so itself if deemed necessary.

In protecting insured deposits, the FDIC is charged with resolving the problems of insured depository institutions at the least possible cost to the deposit insurance fund. In carrying out this responsibility the FDIC engages in several activities, including paying off deposits, arranging the purchase of assets and assumption of liabilities of failed institutions, effecting insured deposit transfers between institutions, creating and operating temporary bridge banks until a resolution can be accomplished, and using its conservatorship powers.

National Credit Union Administration

The National Credit Union Administration, established by the Federal Credit Union Act (Section 1752a) of Congress in 1934, is the agency that supervises the nation's federal credit union system. A three-member bipartisan board appointed by the President for six-year terms manages the National Credit Union Administration. The President also selects a member to serve as Chair of the board.

The main responsibilities of the National Credit Union Administration are the following:

- charter, examine, and supervise more than 4,700 federal credit unions nationwide;

- administer the National Credit Union Share Insurance Fund (NCUSIF), which insures member share accounts in more than

7,600 U.S. federal and state-chartered credit unions; and

- manage the Central Liquidity Facility, a central bank for credit unions, which provides liquidity to the credit union system.

The National Credit Union Administration also has statutory authority to examine and supervise NCUSIF-insured, state-chartered credit unions in coordination with state agencies.

The National Credit Union Administration has five regional offices across the United States that administer its responsibility to charter and supervise credit unions. Its examiners conduct on-site examinations and supervision of each federal credit union and selected state-chartered credit unions. The National Credit Union Administration is funded by the credit unions it regulates and insures.

Comptroller of the Currency
Administrator of National Banks

US Department of the Treasury

Office of the Comptroller of the Currency

The Office of the Comptroller of the Currency (OCC) is the oldest federal bank regulatory agency, established as a bureau of the Treasury Department by the National Currency Act of 1863. It is headed by the Comptroller of the Currency, who is appointed to a five-year term by the President with the advice and consent of the Senate. The Comptroller is also a Director of the FDIC and a Director of the Neighborhood Reinvestment Corporation.

The OCC was created by Congress to charter, regulate, and supervise national banks. The OCC regulates and supervises 1,531 national banks and trust companies and 51 federal branches of foreign banks in the United States, accounting for nearly 70 percent of the total assets of all U.S. commercial banks and branches of foreign banks.

The OCC seeks to ensure that national banks soundly manage their risks, comply with applicable laws, compete effectively with other providers of financial services, offer products and services that meet the needs of customers, and provide fair access to financial services and fair treatment of their customers. The OCC's mission-critical programs include:

- Chartering national banks and issuing interpretations related to permissible banking activities.

- Establishing and communicating regulations, policies, and operating guidance applicable to national banks.

- Supervising the national banking system through on-site examinations, off-site monitoring, systemic risk analyses, and appropriate enforcement activities.

To meet its objectives, the OCC maintains a nationwide staff of bank examiners and other professional and support personnel. Headquartered in Washington, D.C., the OCC has four district offices in Chicago, Dallas, Denver, and New York. In addition, the OCC maintains a network of 50 field offices and 22 satellite locations in cities throughout the United States, as well as resident examiner teams in the 18 largest national banking companies and an examining office in London, England.

The Comptroller receives advice on policy and operational issues from an Executive Committee, comprised of senior agency officials who lead major business units.

The OCC is funded primarily by semiannual assessments on national banks, interest revenue from its investment in U.S. Treasury securities, and other fees. The OCC does not receive congressional appropriations for any of its operations.

Office of Thrift Supervision

The Office of Thrift Supervision was established as a bureau of the U. S. Department of the Treasury in 1989. The Office of Thrift Supervision charters and is the primary regulator for all federal savings associations, and shares joint responsibility with state authorities for supervision of all state savings associations. The Office of Thrift Supervision is also the primary regulator for all savings and loan holding companies.

The mission of the Office of Thrift Supervision is to supervise savings associations and their holding companies in order to maintain their safety and soundness and compliance with consumer laws, and to encourage a competitive industry that meets America's financial service needs.

The Office of Thrift Supervision carries out its mission by (1) adopting regulations governing the thrift institution industry, (2) examining and supervising savings associations and their affiliates, (3) taking appropriate action to enforce compliance with federal laws and regulations, and (4) acting on applications to charter or acquire a savings association. The Office of Thrift Supervision also has the authority to regulate, examine, supervise, and take enforcement action against savings and loan holding companies and other affiliates, as well as entities that provide services to savings associations.

The Office of Thrift Supervision is headed by a Director appointed by the President, with the advice and consent of the Senate, to serve a five-year term. The Director determines policy for the Office of Thrift Supervision and makes final decisions on regulations governing the industry as a whole and on measures affecting individual institutions. The Director also serves as a Director of the Federal Deposit Insurance Corporation and as a Director of the Neighborhood Reinvestment Corporation.

The agency conducts its operations from its headquarters in Washington, D.C., and four regional offices located in Jersey City, New Jersey (Northeast Region); Atlanta, Georgia (Southeast Region); Chicago, Illinois (Central Region); and Dallas, Texas (Western Region).

The Office of Thrift Supervision uses no congressional appropriations to fund any of its operations. It draws its revenues primarily through fees and assessments levied on the institutions it regulates.

ASSETS, LIABILITIES, AND NET WORTH of U.S. Commercial Banks, Thrift Institutions, and Credit Unions as of December 31, 2009[1]

Billions of dollars

Item	Total	U.S. Commercial Banks[2] National	State Member	State Non-Member	U.S. Branches and Agencies of Foreign Banks[5]	Thrift Institutions OTS-Regulated[4] Federal Charter	State Charter	Other FDIC-Supervised Savings Banks	Credit Unions[3] Federal Charter	State Charter
Total assets	15,899	8,196	1,687	1,956	1,913	930	12	321	482	402
Total loans and receivables (net)	8,108	4,139	855	1,288	489	563	8	200	308	258
Loans secured by real estate[6]	4,811	2,398	552	875	39	450	8	179	164	146
Consumer loans[7]	1,316	732	59	185	0	74	0	7	147	112
Commercial and industrial loans	1,508	781	180	195	280	51	0	15	2	4
All other loans and lease receivables[8]	710	385	88	65	170	0	0	2	0	0
LESS: Allowance for possible loan and lease losses	237	157	24	32	0	12	0	3	5	4
Federal funds sold and securities purchased under agreements to resell	478	362	18	22	64	7	0	5	0	0
Cash and due from depository institutions[9]	1,511	609	232	135	324	51	1	21	75	63
Securities and other obligations[10]	2,820	1,499	341	358	178	234	2	69	77	62
U.S. government obligations[11]	717	178	57	99	52	161	2	54	64	50
Obligations of state and local governments[12]	163	76	25	53	0	5	0	4	0	0
Other securities	1,940	1,245	259	206	126	68	0	11	13	12
Other assets[13]	2,982	1,587	241	153	858	75	1	26	22	19
Total liabilities	14,344	7,272	1,494	1,743	1,912	831	10	285	434	363
Total deposits and shares[14]	11,086	5,616	1,222	1,492	1,109	650	9	234	409	345
Federal funds purchased and securities sold under agreements to repurchase	803	432	67	51	200	43	0	10	0	0
Other borrowings[15]	1,565	775	134	175	284	122	1	38	21	15
Other liabilities[16]	890	449	71	25	319	16	0	3	4	3
Net worth[17]	1,555	924	193	213	2	99	2	35	48	39
Memorandum: Number of institutions reporting	15,789	1,459	832	4,532	239	701	64	408	4,714	2,840

Footnotes to Tables

1. The table covers institutions, including those in Puerto Rico and U.S. territories and possessions, insured by the Federal Deposit Insurance Corporation or National Credit Union Savings Insurance Fund. All branches and agencies of foreign banks in the United States, but excluding any in Puerto Rico and U.S. territories and possessions, are covered whether or not insured. Excludes Edge Act and agreement corporations that are not subsidiaries of U.S. commercial banks.

2. Reflects fully consolidated statements of FDIC-insured U.S. banks—including their foreign branches, foreign subsidiaries, branches in Puerto Rico and U.S. territories and possessions, and FDIC insured banks in Puerto Rico and U.S. territories and possessions. Excludes bank holding companies.

3. Data are for federally insured natural person credit unions only.

4. Data for thrift institutions regulated by the OTS reflects fully consolidated statements of condition and operations. Data for OTS regulated thrifts owned directly by other thrifts are excluded to avoid double counting results already included in the parents financial statements.

5. These institutions are not required to file reports of income.

6. Includes loans secured by residential property, commercial property, farmland (including improvements) and unim- proved land; and construction loans secured by real estate.

7. Includes loans, except those secured by real estate, to individuals for household, family, and other personal expenditures including both installment and single payment loans. Net of unearned income on installment loans.

8. Includes loans to financial institutions, for purchasing or carrying securities, to finance agricultural production and other loans to farmers (except those secured by real estate), to states and political subdivisions and public authorities, and miscellaneous types of loans.

Notes continue on the next page

INCOME AND EXPENSES of U.S. Commercial Banks and Thrift Institutions for the Twelve Months Ending December 31, 2009[1]

Billions of dollars

Item	Total	U.S. Commercial Banks[2]			Thrift Institutions			Credit Unions[3]	
					OTS-Regulated[4]		Other FDIC-Super-vised Savings Banks		
		National	State Member	State Non-Member	Federal Charter	State Charter		Federal Charter	State Charter
Operating income	866	506	99	119	70	0	16	31	25
Interest and fees on loans	450	240	43	78	42	0	11	20	16
Other interest and dividend income	137	87	16	15	11	0	3	3	2
All other operating income	277	178	40	25	17	0	2	8	7
Operating expenses	838	484	96	123	67	0	15	29	24
Salaries and benefits	178	104	23	24	10	0	4	7	6
Interest on deposits and shares	113	47	12	25	12	0	4	7	6
Interest on other borrowed money	50	27	5	6	8	0	2	1	1
Provision for loan and lease losses	260	168	26	35	20	0	2	5	4
All other operating expenses	238	138	30	34	17	0	3	9	7
Net operating income	28	22	3	-4	3	0	1	2	1
Securities gains and losses	-2	3	-4	0	0	0	0	-1	0
Extraordinary Items	-4	0	-4	0	0	0	0	0	0
Income taxes	7	4	0	0	3	0	0	0	0
Net income	13	20	-4	-5	0	0	0	1	1
Memorandum: Number of institutions reporting	15,550	1,459	832	4,532	701	64	408	4,714	2,840

9. Includes vault cash, cash items in process of collection, and balances with U.S. and foreign banks and other depository institutions (including demand and time deposits and certificates of deposit for all categories of institutions).

10. Includes government and corporate securities, including mortgage-backed securities and obligations of states and political subdivisions and of U.S. government agencies and corporations.

11. U.S. Treasury securities and securities of, and loans to, U.S. government agencies and corporations.

12. Securities issued by states and political subdivisions and public authorities, except for savings and loan associations and U.S. branches and agencies of foreign banks that do not report these securities separately. Loans to states and political subdivisions and public authorities are included in "All other loans and lease receivables."

13. Customers' liabilities on acceptances, real property owned, various accrual accounts, and miscellaneous assets. For U.S. branches and agencies of foreign banks, also includes net due from head office and other related institutions. For SAIF-insured institutions, also includes equity investment in service corporation subsidiaries.

14. Includes demand, savings, and time deposits, (including certificates of deposit at commercial banks, U.S. branches and agencies of foreign banks, and savings banks), credit balances at U.S. agencies of foreign banks and share balances at savings and loan associations and credit unions (including certificates of deposit, NOW accounts, and share draft accounts). For U.S. commercial banks, includes deposits in foreign offices, branches in U.S. territories and possessions, and Edge Act and Agreement corporation subsidiaries.

15. Includes interest-bearing demand notes

issued to the U.S. Treasury, borrowing from Federal Reserve Banks and Federal Home Loan Banks, subordinated debt, limited life preferred stock, and other nondeposit borrowing.

16. Includes depository institutions' own mortgage borrowing, liability for capitalized leases, liability on acceptances executed, various accrual accounts, and miscellaneous liabilities. For U.S. branches and agencies of foreign banks, also includes net owed to head office and other related institutions.

17. Includes capital stock, surplus, capital reserves, and undivided profits.

NOTE: Data are rounded to nearest billion. Consequently, some information may not reconcile precisely. Additionally, balances less than $500 million will show as zero.

Federal Financial Institutions Examination Council Act

12 U.S.C. § 3301. *Declaration of purpose*

It is the purpose of this chapter to establish a Financial Institutions Examination Council which shall prescribe uniform principles and standards for the Federal examination of financial institutions by the Office of the Comptroller of the Currency, the Federal Deposit Insurance Corporation, the Board of Governors of the Federal Reserve System, the Federal Home Loan Bank Board, and the National Credit Union Administration and make recommendations to promote uniformity in the supervision of these financial institutions. The Council's actions shall be designed to promote consistency in such examination and to insure progressive and vigilant supervision.

12 U.S.C. § 3302. *Definitions*

As used in this chapter—

(1) the term "Federal financial institutions regulatory agencies" means the Office of the Comptroller of the Currency, the Board of Governors of the Federal Reserve System, the Federal Deposit Insurance Corporation, the Office of Thrift Supervision, and the National Credit Union Administration;

(2) the term "Council" means the Financial Institutions Examination Council; and

(3) the term "financial institution" means a commercial bank, a savings bank, a trust company, a savings association, a building and loan association, a homestead association, a cooperative bank, or a credit union.

12 U.S.C. § 3303. *Financial Institutions Examination Council*

(a) Establishment; composition

There is established the Financial Institutions Examination Council which shall consist of—

(1) the Comptroller of the Currency,

(2) the Chairman of the Board of Directors of the Federal Deposit Insurance Corporation,

(3) a Governor of the Board of Governors of the Federal Reserve System designated by the Chairman of the Board,

(4) the Director, Office of Thrift Supervision,

(5) the Chairman of the National Credit Union Administration Board; and

(6) the Chairman of the State Liaison Committee

(b) Chairmanship

The members of the Council shall select the first chairman of the Council. Thereafter the chairmanship shall rotate among the members of the Council.

(c) Term of office

The term of the Chairman of the Council shall be two years.

(d) Designation of officers and employees

The members of the Council may, from time to time, designate other officers or employees of their respective agencies to carry out their duties on the Council.

(e) Compensation and expenses

Each member of the Council shall serve without additional compensation but shall be entitled to reason-able expenses incurred while carrying out his official duties as such a member.

12 U.S.C. § 3304. *Costs and expenses of Council*

One-fifth of the costs and expenses of the Council, including the salaries of its employees, shall be paid by each of the Federal financial institutions regulatory agencies. Annual assessments for such share shall be levied by the Council based upon its projected budget for the year, and additional assessments may be made during the year, if necessary.

12 U.S.C. § 3305. *Functions of Council*

(a) Establishment of principles and standards

The Council shall establish uniform principles and standards and report forms for the examination of financial institutions which shall be applied by the Federal financial institutions regulatory agencies.

(b) Making recommendations regarding supervisory matters and adequacy of supervisory tools

(1) The Council shall make recommendations for uniformity in other supervisory matters, such as, but not limited to, classifying loans subject to country risk, identifying financial institutions in need of special supervisory attention, and evaluating the soundness of large loans that are shared by two or more financial institutions. In addition, the Council shall make recommendations regarding the adequacy of supervisory tools for determining the impact of holding company operations on the financial institutions within the holding company and shall consider the ability of supervisory agencies to discover possi-

ble fraud or questionable and illegal payments and practices which might occur in the operation of financial institutions or their holding companies.

(2) When a recommendation of the Council is found unacceptable by one or more of the applicable Federal financial institutions regulatory agencies, the agency or agencies shall submit to the Council, within a time period specified by the Council, a written statement of the reasons the recommendation is unacceptable.

(c) Development of uniform reporting system

The Council shall develop uniform reporting systems for federally supervised financial institutions, their holding companies, and non-financial institution subsidiaries of such institutions or holding companies. The authority to develop uniform reporting systems shall not restrict or amend the requirements of section 78l(i) of Title 15.

(d) Conducting schools for examiners and assistant examiners

The Council shall conduct schools for examiners and assistant examiners employed by the Federal financial institutions regulatory agencies. Such schools shall be open to enrollment by employees of State financial institutions supervisory agencies and employees of the Federal Housing Finance Board under conditions specified by the Council.

(e) Affect on Federal regulatory agency research and development of new financial institutions supervisory agencies

Nothing in this chapter shall be construed to limit or discourage Federal regulatory agency research and development of new financial institutions supervisory methods and tools, nor to preclude the field testing of any innovation devised by any Federal regulatory agency.

(f) Annual report

Not later than April 1 of each year, the Council shall prepare an annual report covering its activities during the preceding year.

(g) Flood insurance

The Council shall consult with and assist the Federal entities for lending regulation, as such term is defined in section 4121(a) of Title 42, in developing and coordinating uniform standards and requirements for use by regulated lending institutions under the national flood insurance program.

12 U.S.C. § 3306. State liaison

To encourage the application of uniform examination principles and standards by State and Federal supervisory agencies, the Council shall establish a liaison committee composed of five representatives of State agencies which supervise financial institutions which shall meet at least twice a year with the Council. Members of the liaison committee shall receive a reasonable allowance for necessary expenses incurred in attending meetings.

Members of the Liaison Committee shall elect a chairperson from among the members serving on the committee.

12 U.S.C. § 3307. Administration

(a) Authority of Chairman of Council

The Chairman of the Council is authorized to carry out and to delegate the authority to carry out the internal administration of the Council, including the appointment and supervision of employees and the distribution of business among members, employees, and administrative units.

(b) Use of personnel, services, and facilities of Federal financial institutions regulatory agencies, Federal Reserve banks, and Federal Home Loan Banks.

In addition to any other authority

conferred upon it by this chapter, in carrying out its functions under this chapter, the Council may utilize, with their consent and to the extent practical, the personnel, services, and facilities of the Federal financial institutions regulatory agencies, Federal Reserve banks, and Federal Home Loan Banks, with or without reimbursement therefore.

(c) Compensation, authority, and duties of officers and employees; experts and consultants

In addition, the Council may—

(1) subject to the provisions of Title 5 relating to the competitive service, classification, and General Schedule pay rates, appoint and fix the compensation of such officers and employees as are necessary to carry out the provisions of this chapter, and to prescribe the authority and duties of such officers and employees; and

(2) obtain the services of such experts and consultants as are necessary to carry out the provisions of this chapter.

12 U.S.C. § 3308. Access to books, accounts, records, etc., by Council

For the purpose of carrying out this chapter, the Council shall have access to all books, accounts, records, reports, files, memorandums, papers, things, and property belonging to or in use by Federal financial institutions regulatory agencies, including reports of examination of financial institutions or their holding companies from whatever source, together with workpapers and correspondence files related to such reports, whether or not a part of the report, and all without any deletions.

12 U.S.C. § 3309. Risk management training

(a) Seminars

The Council shall develop and administer training seminars in risk management for its employees and the employees of insured financial institutions.

(b) Study of risk management training program

Not later than end of the 1-year period beginning on August 9, 1989, the Council shall—

(1) conduct a study on the feasibility and appropriateness of establishing a formalized risk management training program designed to lead to the certification of Risk Management Analysts; and

(2) report to the Congress the results of such study.

12 U.S.C. § 3310. Establishment of Appraisal Subcommittee

There shall be within the Council a subcommittee to be known as the "Appraisal Subcommittee," which shall consist of the designees of the heads of the Federal financial institutions regulatory agencies. Each such designee shall be a person who has demonstrated knowledge and competence concerning the appraisal profession.

12 U.S.C. § 3311. Required review of regulations

(a) In general

Not less frequently than once every 10 years, the Council and each appropriate Federal banking agency represented on the Council shall conduct a review of all regulations prescribed by the Council or by any such appropriate Federal banking agency, respectively, in order to identify outdated or otherwise unnecessary regulatory requirements imposed on insured depository institutions.

(b) Process

In conducting the review under subsection (a) of this section, the Council or the appropriate Federal banking agency shall—

(1) categorize the regulations described in subsection (a) of this section by type (such as consumer regulations, safety and soundness regulations, or such other designations as determined by the Council, or the appropriate Federal banking agency); and

(2) at regular intervals, provide notice and solicit public comment on a particular category or categories of regulations, requesting commentators to identify areas of the regulations that are outdated, unnecessary, or unduly burdensome.

(c) Complete review

The Council or the appropriate Federal banking agency shall ensure that the notice and comment period described in subsection (b)(2) of this section is conducted with respect to all regulations described in subsection (a) of this section not less frequently than once every 10 years.

(d) Regulatory response

The Council or the appropriate Federal banking agency shall—

(1) publish in the *Federal Register* a summary of the comments received under this section, identifying significant issues raised and providing comment on such issues; and

(2) eliminate unnecessary regulations to the extent that such action is appropriate.

(e) Report to Congress

Not later than 30 days after carrying out subsection (d)(1) of this section, the Council shall submit to Congress a report, which shall include—

(1) a summary of any significant issues raised by public comments received by the Council and the appropriate Federal banking agencies under this section and the relative merits of such issues; and

(2) an analysis of whether the appropriate Federal banking agency involved is able to address the regulatory burdens associated with such issues by regulation, or whether such burdens must be addressed by legislative action.

Excerpts from Statute Governing Appraisal Subcommittee

12 U.S.C. § 3332. Functions of Appraisal Subcommittee

(a) In general

The Appraisal Subcommittee shall—

(1) monitor the requirements established by States for the certification and licensing of individuals who are qualified to perform appraisals in connection with federally related transactions, including a code of professional responsibility;

(2) monitor the requirements established by the Federal financial institutions regulatory agencies and the Resolution Trust Corporation with respect to—

(A) appraisal standards for federally related transactions under their jurisdiction, and

(B) determinations as to which federally related transactions under their jurisdiction require the services of a State certified appraiser and which require the services of a State licensed appraiser;

(3) maintain a national registry of State certified and licensed appraisers who are eligible to perform appraisals in federally related transactions; and

(4) Omitted.

(b) Monitoring and reviewing Foundation

The Appraisal Subcommittee shall monitor and review the practices, procedures, activities, and organizational structure of the Appraisal Foundation.

12 U.S.C. § 3333. Chairperson of Appraisal Subcommittee; term of Chairperson; meetings

(a) Chairperson

The Council shall select the Chairperson of the subcommittee. The term of the Chairperson shall be two years.

Excerpts from Home Mortgage Disclosure Act

12 U.S.C. § 2801. Congressional findings and declaration of purpose

(a) Findings of Congress

The Congress finds that some depository institutions have sometimes contributed to the decline of certain geographic areas by their failure pursuant to their chartering responsibilities to provide adequate home financing to qualified applicants on reasonable terms and conditions.

(b) Purpose of chapter

The purpose of this chapter is to provide the citizens and public officials of the United States with sufficient information to enable them to determine whether depository institutions are filling their obligations to serve the housing needs of the communities and neighborhoods in which they are located and to assist public officials in their determination of the distribution of public sector investments in a manner designed to improve the private investment environment.

(c) Construction of chapter

Nothing in this chapter is intended to, nor shall it be construed to, encourage unsound lending practices or the allocation of credit.

12 U.S.C. § 2803. Maintenance of records and public disclosure

(f) Data disclosure system; operation, etc.

The Federal Financial Institutions Examination Council, in consultation with the Secretary, shall implement a system to facilitate access to data required to be disclosed under this section. Such system shall include arrangements for a central depository of data in each primary metropolitan statistical area, metropolitan statistical area, or consolidated metropolitan statistical area that is not comprised of designated primary metropolitan statistical areas. Disclosure statements shall be made available to the public for inspection and copying at such central depository of data for all depository institutions which are required to disclose information under this section (or which are exempted pursuant to section 2805(b) of this title) and which have a home office or branch office within such primary metropolitan statistical area, metropolitan statistical area, or consolidated metropolitan statistical area that is not comprised of designated primary metropolitan statistical areas.

12 U.S.C. § 2809. Compilation of aggregate data

(a) Commencement; scope of data and tables

Beginning with data for calendar year 1980, the Federal Financial Institutions Examination Council shall compile each year, for each primary metropolitan statistical area, metropolitan statistical area, or consolidated metropolitan statistical area that is not comprised of designated primary metropolitan statistical areas, aggregate data by census tract for all depository institutions which are required to disclose data under section 2803 of this title or which are exempt pursuant to section 2805(b) of this title. The Council shall also produce tables indicating, for each primary metropolitan statistical area, metropolitan statistical area, or consolidated metropolitan statistical area that is not comprised of designated primary metropolitan statistical areas, aggregate lending patterns for various categories of census tracts grouped according to location, age of housing stock, income level, and racial characteristics.

(b) Staff and data processing resources

The Board shall provide staff and data processing resources to the Council to enable it to carry out the provisions of subsection (a) of this section.

(c) Availability to public

The data and tables required pursuant to subsection (a) of this section shall be made available to the public no later than December 31 of the year following the calendar year on which the data is based.

Excerpts from S.A.F.E. Mortgage Licensing Act

12 U.S.C. § 5101. Purposes and methods for establishing a mortgage licensing system and registry

In order to increase uniformity, reduce regulatory burden, enhance consumer protection, and reduce fraud, the States, through the Conference of State Bank Supervisors and the American Association of Residential Mortgage Regulators, are hereby encouraged to establish a Nationwide Mortgage Licensing System and Registry for the residential mortgage industry that accomplishes all of the following objectives:

(1) Provides uniform license applications and reporting requirements for State-licensed loan originators.

(2) Provides a comprehensive licensing and supervisory database.

(3) Aggregates and improves the flow of information to and between regulators.

(4) Provides increased accountability and tracking of loan originators.

(5) Streamlines the licensing

process and reduces the regulatory burden.

(6) Enhances consumer protections and supports anti-fraud measures.

(7) Provides consumers with easily accessible information, offered at no charge, utilizing electronic media, including the Internet, regarding the employment history of, and publicly adjudicated disciplinary and enforcement actions against, loan originators.

(8) Establishes a means by which residential mortgage loan originators would, to the greatest extent possible, be required to act in the best interests of the consumer.

(9) Facilitates responsible behavior in the subprime mortgage market place and provides comprehensive training and examination requirements related to subprime mortgage lending.

(10) Facilitates the collection and disbursement of consumer complaints on behalf of State and Federal mortgage regulators.

12 U.S.C. § 5106. System of registration administration by Federal agencies

(a) Development

(1) In general

The Federal banking agencies shall jointly, through the Federal Financial Institutions Examination Council, and together with the Farm Credit Administration, develop and maintain a system for registering employees of a depository institution, employees of a subsidiary that is owned and controlled by a depository institution and regulated by a Federal banking agency, or employee of an institution regulated by the Farm Credit Administration, as registered loan originators with the Nationwide Mortgage Licensing System and Registry. The system shall be implemented before the end of the 1-year period beginning on the date of enactment of this title.

(2) Registration requirements

In connection with the registration of any loan originator under this subsection, the appropriate Federal banking agency and the Farm Credit Administration shall, at a minimum, furnish or cause to be furnished to the Nationwide Mortgage Licensing System and Registry information concerning the employees' identity, including—

(A) fingerprints for submission to the Federal Bureau of Investigation, and any governmental agency or entity authorized to receive such information for a State and national criminal history background check; and

(B) personal history and experience, including authorization for the Nationwide Mortgage Licensing System and Registry to obtain information related to any administrative, civil or criminal findings by any governmental jurisdiction.

(b) Coordination

(1) Unique identifier

The Federal banking agencies, through the Financial Institutions Examination Council, and the Farm Credit Administration shall coordi-nate with the Nationwide Mortgage Licensing System and Registry to establish protocols for assigning a unique identifier to each registered loan originator that will facilitate electronic tracking and uniform identification of, and public access to, the employment history of and publicly adjudicated disciplinary and enforcement actions against loan originators.

(2) Nationwide Mortgage Licensing System and Registry development

To facilitate the transfer of information required by subsection (a)(2), the Nationwide Mortgage Licensing System and Registry shall coordinate with the Federal banking agencies, through the Financial Institutions Examination Council, and the Farm Credit Administration concerning the development and operation, by such System and Registry, of the registration functionality and data requirements for loan originators.

(c) Consideration of factors and procedures

In establishing the registration procedures under subsection (a) and the protocols for assigning a unique identifier to a registered loan originator, the Federal banking agencies shall make such de minimis exceptions as may be appropriate to paragraphs (1)(A) and (2) of section 5103(a) of this title, shall make reasonable efforts to utilize existing information to minimize the burden of registering loan originators, and shall consider methods for automating the process to the greatest extent practicable consistent with the purposes of this title.

Deloitte.

Deloitte & Touche LLP
Suite 800
1750 Tysons Boulevard
McLean, VA 22102-4219
USA

Tel: +1 703 251 1000
Fax: +1 703 251 3400
www.deloitte.com

INDEPENDENT AUDITORS' REPORT

The Federal Financial Institutions Examination Council:

We have audited the accompanying balance sheets of the Federal Financial Institutions Examination Council (the "Council") as of December 31, 2009 and 2008, and the related statements of revenues and expenses and changes in cumulative results of operations, and cash flows for the years then ended. These financial statements are the responsibility of the Council's management. Our responsibility is to express an opinion on these financial statements based on our audits.

We conducted our audits in accordance with auditing standards generally accepted in the United States of America and the standards applicable to financial audits contained in *Government Auditing Standards* issued by the Comptroller General of the United States. Those standards require that we plan and perform the audit to obtain reasonable assurance about whether the respective financial statements are free of material misstatement. An audit includes consideration of internal control over financial reporting as a basis for designing audit procedures that are appropriate in the circumstances, but not for the purpose of expressing an opinion on the effectiveness of the Council's internal control over financial reporting. Accordingly, we express no such opinion. An audit also includes examining, on a test basis, evidence supporting the amounts and disclosures in the respective financial statements, assessing the accounting principles used and significant estimates made by management, as well as evaluating the overall financial statement presentation. We believe that our audits provide a reasonable basis for our opinion.

In our opinion, such financial statements present fairly, in all material respects, the financial position of the Federal Financial Institutions Examination Council as of December 31, 2009 and 2008, and the results of its operations and its cash flows for the years then ended in conformity with accounting principles generally accepted in the United States of America.

In accordance with *Government Auditing Standards*, we have also issued our report dated March 9, 2010, on our consideration of the Council's internal control over financial reporting and our tests of its compliance with certain provisions of laws, regulations, contracts, and grant agreements and other matters. The purpose of that report is to describe the scope of our testing of internal control over financial reporting and compliance and the results of that testing, and not to provide an opinion on the internal control over financial reporting or on compliance. That report is an integral part of an audit performed in accordance with *Government Auditing Standards* and should be considered in assessing the results of our audit.

Deloitte + Touche LLP

McLean, VA
March 9, 2010

Member of
Deloitte Touche Tohmatsu

33

FEDERAL FINANCIAL INSTITUTIONS EXAMINATION COUNCIL
Balance Sheets

	As of December 31,	
	2009	2008

ASSETS
CURRENT ASSETS

Cash	$ 1,022,700	$ 708,677
Accounts receivable from member organizations (Note 3)	1,001,002	1,572,136
Other accounts receivable—net	90,628	105,623
Total current assets	2,114,330	2,386,436

CAPITAL ASSETS

Furniture and equipment—at cost	118,390	24,199
Central Data Repository—at cost (Note 4)	18,231,272	16,036,559
HMDA Software—at cost (Note 5)	2,344,680	1,544,895
Less accumulated depreciation	(10,827,552)	(7,887,093)
Net capital assets	9,866,790	9,718,560
TOTAL ASSETS	$ 11,981,120	$ 12,104,996

LIABILITIES AND CUMULATIVE RESULTS OF OPERATIONS

CURRENT LIABILITIES

Accounts payable and accrued liabilities payable to member organizations (Note 3)	$ 981,180	$ 1,300,718
Other accounts payable and accrued liabilities (Note 4)	927,051	652,538
Accrued payroll and annual leave	20,117	22,008
Capital lease payable (Note 7)	16,815	–
Deferred revenue (Note 4)	1,856,180	3,388,881
Total current liabilities	3,801,343	5,364,145

LONG-TERM LIABILITIES

Capital lease payable (Note 7)	80,576	–
Deferred revenue (Notes 4 and 5)	7,913,219	6,579,680
Total long-term liabilities	7,993,795	6,579,680
Total liabilities	11,795,138	11,943,825
CUMULATIVE RESULTS OF OPERATIONS	185,982	161,171
TOTAL LIABILITIES AND CUMULATIVE RESULTS OF OPERATIONS	$ 11,981,120	$ 12,104,996

See notes to financial statements.

FEDERAL FINANCIAL INSTITUTIONS EXAMINATION COUNCIL
Statements of Revenues and Expenses and Changes in Cumulative Results of Operations

	For the years ended December 31,	
	2009	2008
REVENUES		
Assessments on member organizations (Note 3)	$ 589,988	$ 574,447
Central Data Repository (Note 4)	5,741,157	6,160,478
Home Mortgage Disclosure (Note 5)	3,071,973	2,969,535
Tuition (Note 3)	2,322,041	1,744,029
Community Reinvestment Act (Note 5)	1,013,110	931,244
Uniform Bank Performance Report (Note 5)	537,606	565,522
Appraisal Subcommittee (Note 5)	–	178,963
Total revenues	13,275,875	13,124,218
EXPENSES		
Data processing	4,370,506	4,126,928
Professional fees (Note 4)	3,674,379	4,261,260
Salaries and related benefits (Note 3)	1,468,414	1,164,304
Depreciation (Note 4)	2,943,660	2,497,774
Rental of office space (Note 6)	247,648	454,184
Administration fees (Note 3)	245,000	190,400
Travel	156,742	135,006
Books and subscriptions	18,985	16,255
Other seminar expenses	33,343	30,824
Rental and maintenance of office equipment	50,967	41,998
Office and other supplies	14,107	33,980
Printing	19,342	43,261
Postage	1,960	2,475
Miscellaneous	6,011	9,042
Total expenses	13,251,064	13,007,691
RESULTS OF OPERATIONS	24,811	116,527
CUMULATIVE RESULTS OF OPERATIONS—Beginning of year	161,171	44,644
CUMULATIVE RESULTS OF OPERATIONS—End of year	$ 185,982	$ 161,171

See notes to financial statements.

FEDERAL FINANCIAL INSTITUTIONS EXAMINATION COUNCIL
Statements of Cash Flows

	For the years ended December 31,	
	2009	2008
CASH FLOWS FROM OPERATING ACTIVITIES		
Results of operations	$ 24,811	$ 116,527
Adjustments to reconcile results of operations to net cash provided by operating activities:		
Depreciation	2,943,660	2,497,774
Central Data Repository write-off	–	1,068,697
(Increase) decrease in assets:		
Accounts receivable from member organizations	571,133	41,730
Other accounts receivable	14,995	151,274
Increase (decrease) in liabilities:		
Accounts payable and accrued liabilities payable to member organizations	(319,538)	151,924
Other accounts payable and accrued liabilities	642,017	(598,992)
Accrued payroll and annual leave	(1,891)	(209,443)
Deferred revenue (current and non-current)	(199,161)	(552,620)
Deferred rent	–	(32,515)
Net cash provided by operating activities	3,676,026	2,634,356
CASH FLOWS FROM INVESTING ACTIVITIES		
Capital expenditures	(3,362,003)	(2,763,850)
NET (DECREASE) INCREASE IN CASH	314,023	(129,494)
CASH BALANCE—Beginning of year	708,677	838,171
CASH BALANCE—End of year	$ 1,022,700	$ 708,677

See notes to financial statements.

1. Organization and Purpose

The Federal Financial Institutions Examination Council (the "Council") was established under Title X of the Financial Institutions Regulatory and Interest Rate Control Act of 1978. The purpose of the Council is to prescribe uniform principles and standards for the federal examination of financial institutions and to make recommendations to promote uniformity in the supervision of these financial institutions. The five agencies which are represented on the Council, referred to hereinafter as member organizations, are as follows:

> Board of Governors of the Federal Reserve System (FRB)
> Federal Deposit Insurance Corporation (FDIC)
> National Credit Union Administration (NCUA)
> Office of the Comptroller of the Currency (OCC)
> Office of Thrift Supervision (OTS)

In accordance with the Financial Services Regulatory Relief Act of 2006, a representative state regulator was added as a full voting member of the Council in October 2006.

The Council was given additional statutory responsibilities by section 340 of the Housing and Community Development Act of 1980, Public Law 96-399. Among these responsibilities are the implementation of a system to facilitate public access to data that depository institutions must disclose under the Home Mortgage Disclosure Act of 1975 (HMDA) and the aggregation of annual HMDA data, by census tract, for each metropolitan statistical area.

Appraisal Subcommittee—The Council's financial statements do not include financial data for the Council's Appraisal Subcommittee (the Subcommittee). The Subcommittee was created pursuant to Public Law 101–73, Title XI of the Financial Institutions Reform, Recovery, and Enforcement Act of 1989. The functions of the Appraisal Subcommittee are related to the certification and licensing of individuals who perform appraisals in connection with federally related real estate transactions. Members of the Appraisal Subcommittee consist of the designees of the heads of those agencies, which comprise the Council and the designee of the head of the Department of Housing and Urban Development.

All functions and responsibilities assigned to the Council under Title XI are performed directly by the Appraisal Subcommittee without any need for approval or concurrence from the Council. The Appraisal Subcommittee has its own policies and procedures and submits its own Annual Report to the President of the Senate and Speaker of the House. The Council is not responsible for any debts incurred by the Subcommittee, nor are Subcommittee funds available for use by the Council.

2. Significant Accounting Policies

The Council prepares its financial statements in accordance with accounting principles generally accepted in the United States of America (GAAP).

Revenues—Assessments made on member organizations are to fund its operations based on expected cash needs. Amounts over- or under-assessed due to differences between actual and expected cash needs flow into "Cumulative Results of Operations" during the year and then are used to offset or increase the next year's assessment. Deficits in "Cumulative Results of Operations" can be made up in the following year's assessments.

Tuition revenue is adjusted at year-end to match expenses incurred as a result of providing education classes. Uniform Bank Performance Report (UBPR) revenue is adjusted at year-end to match expenses incurred as a result of providing UBPR service. For differences between revenues and expenses, member agencies are assessed an additional amount or credited a refund based on each member's proportional cost for the Examiner Education and UBPR budget.

Capital Assets—Furniture and equipment is recorded at cost less accumulated depreciation. Depreciation is calculated on a straight-line basis over the estimated useful lives of the assets, which range from four to ten years. Upon the sale or other disposition of a depreciable asset, the cost and related accumulated depreciation are removed and any gain or loss is recognized. The Central Data Repository (CDR), an internally developed software project, is recorded at cost as required by the Internal Use Software Topic of FASB Accounting Standards Codification. (See Note 4)

Deferred Revenue—Deferred revenue includes cash collected and accounts receivable primarily related to the CDR and HMDA. (See Notes 4 and 5)

Deferred Rent—The lease for office and classroom space contains scheduled rent increases over the term of the lease. As required by the Leases Topic of the FASB Accounting Standards Codification, rent abatements and scheduled rent increases must be considered in determining the annual rent expense to be recognized. The deferred rent represents the difference between the actual lease payments and the rent expense recognized.

Estimates—The preparation of financial statements in conformity with GAAP requires management to make estimates and assumptions that affect the reported amounts of assets and liabilities and the disclosure of contingent assets and liabilities at the date of the financial statements and the reported amounts of revenues and expenses during the reporting period. Actual results could differ from those estimates.

Allowance for Doubtful Accounts—Accounts receivable for non-members are shown net of the allowance for doubtful accounts. Accounts receivable considered uncollectible are charged against the allowance account in the year they are deemed uncollectible. The allowance for doubtful accounts is adjusted monthly, based upon a review of outstanding receivables.

Recently Issued Accounting Standards—On June 30, 2009, the FASB issued SFAS No. 168, "The Statement of Financial Accounting Standards Codification and the Hierarchy of Generally Accepted Accounting Principles, a replacement of SFAS No. 162, The Hierarchy of Generally Accepted Accounting Principles" (SFAS 168). SFAS 168 establishes the FASB Accounting Standards Codification (ASC) as the source of authoritative accounting principles recognized by the FASB to be applied by entities in the preparation of financial statements in conformity with GAAP. The ASC does not change current GAAP, but it introduces a new structure that organizes the authoritative standards by topic. SFAS 168 is effective for financial statements issued for periods ending after September 15, 2009. In accordance with the requirements of this standard the ASC is referenced in the Council's financial statements and footnotes.

The Subsequent Events Topic of FASB ASC establishes general standards of accounting for and disclosure of events that occur through the balance sheet date but before financial statements are issued or are available to be issued. The ASC sets forth (i) the period after the balance sheet date during which management of a reporting entity should evaluate events or transactions that may occur for potential recognition or disclosure in the financial statements; (ii) the circumstances under which an entity should recognize events or transactions occurring after the balance sheet date in its financial statements; and (iii) the disclosures that an entity should make about events or transactions that occurred after the balance sheet date, including disclosure of the date through which an entity has evaluated subsequent events and whether that represents the date the financial statements were issued or were available to be issued. The Council adopted the standard for the year ended December 31, 2009.

3. Transactions with Member Organizations

	2009	2008
Accounts Receivable		
Board of Governors of the Federal Reserve System	$ 209,992	$ 373,466
Federal Deposit Insurance Corporation	439,609	466,052
National Credit Union Administration	48,593	109,261
Office of the Comptroller of the Currency	$ 244,883	$ 522,167
Office of Thrift Supervision	57,995	101,190
	$ 1,001,002	$ 1,572,136
Accounts Payable and Accrued Liabilities		
Board of Governors of the Federal Reserve System	$ 618,861	$ 650,672
Federal Deposit Insurance Corporation	247,870	396,899
National Credit Union Administration	20,877	40,085

Notes continue on the following page.

37

	2009	2008
Office of the Comptroller of the Currency	72,103	132,891
Office of Thrift Supervision	21,469	80,171
	$ 981,180	$ 1,300,718

Operations

		2009		2008
Assessments to member organizations for operating expenses	$	589,988	$	574,447
FRB provided administrative support services to the Council at an expense of		245,000		190,400
Member organizations provide office space and data processing services to the Council at an expense of		4,618,154		4,374,577

The Council does not directly employ personnel, but rather member organizations detail personnel to support Council operations. These personnel are paid through the payroll systems of member organizations. Salaries and fringe benefits, including retirement benefit plan contributions, are reimbursed to these organizations. The Council does not have any post-retirement or post-employment benefit liabilities since Council personnel are included in the plans of the member organizations.

Member organizations are not reimbursed for the costs of personnel who serve as Council members and on the various task forces and committees of the Council. The value of these contributed services is not included in the accompanying financial statements.

Examiner Education

The Council provides seminars in the Washington, D.C. area and at regional locations throughout the country for member organization examiners and other agencies. Tuition revenue earned from member organizations was: $2,220,876 $1,627,429

4. **Central Data Repository**

In 2003, the Council entered into an agreement with UNISYS to enhance the methods and systems used to collect, validate, process, and distribute Call Report information, and to store this information in a Central Data Repository (CDR).

The CDR was placed into service in October 2005. At that time, the Council began depreciating the CDR project on the straight-line basis over its estimated useful life of 63 months. In 2009, the Council reevaluated the useful life of CDR and decided to extend the estimated useful life by an additional 36 months based on enhanced functionality of the software. The

Council records depreciation expenses and recognizes the same amount of revenue. The value of the CDR asset as of December 31, 2009 and 2008, includes the fully accrued and paid cost. The accrued costs related to CDR are $204,000 as of December 31, 2009.

	2009	2008
Capital Asset CDR		
Beginning balance	$14,140,655	$12,858,440
Software placed in use during the year	4,090,617	1,282,215
Software in use	18,231,272	14,140,655
Software in development	–	1,895,904
Total asset	$18,231,272	$16,036,559

Other Accounts Payable and Accrued Liabilities

		2009		2008
Payable to UNISYS for the CDR project	$	729,166	$	609,203
Other vendors unrelated to the CDR project		197,885		43,335
Total other accounts payable and accrued liabilities	$	927,051	$	652,538

Revenues—Central Data Repository—The Council is funding the project by billing the three participating Council member organizations (FRB, FDIC, and OCC). Funding for the year ended December 31, 2009 and 2008, is as follows.

	2009	2008
Deferred Revenue		
Beginning balance	$ 8,173,666	$ 9,776,071
Additions	2,194,713	895,369
Less revenue recognized	(2,943,660)	(2,497,774)
Ending balance	$ 7,424,719	$ 8,173,666
Current portion deferred revenue	$ 1,856,180	$ 3,138,881
Long-term deferred revenue	5,568,539	5,034,785
	$ 7,424,719	$ 8,173,666
Total CDR Revenue		
Revenue	$ 2,943,660	$ 2,497,774
Hosting and maintenance fees	2,797,497	3,662,704
Total CDR revenue	$ 5,741,157	$ 6,160,478
Professional Fees		
Hosting and maintenance fees for the CDR project	$ 2,797,497	$ 3,662,704
Other professional fees unrelated to the CDR project	876,882	598,556
Total professional fees	$ 3,674,379	$ 4,261,260

	2009	2008
Depreciation		
Depreciation for the CDR project	$ 2,943,660	$ 2,497,774
Average monthly depreciation	$ 245,305	$ 208,148

5. **Other Revenue**

HMDA—The Council entered into an agreement with FRB to maintain and support the HMDA processing system. In 2007, the Council began a rewrite of the entire HMDA processing system. The total estimated cost for the rewrite is $3.2 million over 4 years. The HMDA rewrite will enhance the processing system. The cost of the software in process is $2,344,680 and $1,544,895 as of December 31, 2009 and 2008, respectively. The accrued costs related to the HMDA rewrite are $65,000 as of December 31, 2009. The financial activity associated with the processing system for the year ended December 31, 2009 and 2008, is as follows.

	2009	2008
HMDA Deferred Revenue		
The Council recognized the following revenue from member organizations for the production and distribution of reports under the HMDA	$ 2,234,514	$ 2,088,052
The Council recognized the following revenue from the Department of Housing and Urban Development's participation in the HMDA project:	559,151	600,089
The Council recognized the following revenue from the Mortgage Insurance Companies of America for performing HMDA-related work	278,308	264,193
The balance of the HMDA revenue for 2009 and 2008 from sales to the public	–	17,201
Total HMDA	$ 3,071,973	$ 2,969,535

Community Reinvestment Act (CRA)—The Council recognized revenue for support of operating expenses from the participating member agencies.

Uniform Bank Performance Report (UBPR)—The Council coordinates the production and distribution of the Uniform Bank Performance Reports (UBPR) through the FDIC. The Council is reimbursed for the direct cost of the operating expenses it incurs for this project. The Council recognized revenue for coordinating and providing certain administrative support to the UBPR project.

Appraisal Subcommittee—The Council recognized revenue in 2008 for providing space to the Appraisal Subcommittee.

6. Operating Leases

The FRB, on behalf of the Council, entered into two operating leases at market value to secure office and classroom space. One lease terminated in 2008. The second lease terminated in 2009. The Council entered into a new lease with the FDIC as of January 2010.

Years ending December 31	Amount
2010	$ 258,385
2011	261,598
2012	264,900
2013	268,292
2014	271,772
Total minimum lease payments	$ 1,324,947

Rental expenses under these operating leases were $247,648 and $454,184 as of December 31, 2009 and 2008, respectively.

7. Capital Leases

In December 2009, the Council entered into a capital lease for printing equipment. The capital lease term extends through 2014. Furniture and equipment includes $97,391 in 2009 for the capital lease. The capital lease will commence in January 2010, when the Council will begin to depreciate the asset and pay interest accordingly. The Council will begin payments towards the capital lease in February 2010.

The future minimum lease payments required under the capital lease and the present value of the net minimum lease payments as of December 31, 2009, are as follows:

Years ending December 31	Amount
2010	$ 24,466
2011	24,466
2012	24,466
2013	24,466
2014	24,467
Total minimum lease payments	$ 122,331
Less amount representing maintenance	(6,000)
Net minimum lease payments	116,331
Less amount representing interest	(18,940)
Net minimum lease payments	97,391
Less current maturities of capital lease payments	(16,815)
Long-term capital lease obligations	$ 80,576

8. Subsequent Events

There were no subsequent events that require adjustments to or disclosures in the financial statements as of December 31, 2009. Subsequent events were evaluated through March 9, 2010, which is the date the Council issued the financial statements.

Deloitte.

Deloitte & Touche LLP
Suite 800
1750 Tysons Boulevard
McLean, VA 22102-4219
USA

Tel: +1 703 251 1000
Fax: +1 703 251 3400
www.deloitte.com

INDEPENDENT AUDITORS' REPORT ON INTERNAL CONTROL OVER FINANCIAL REPORTING AND ON COMPLIANCE AND OTHER MATTERS BASED ON AN AUDIT OF FINANCIAL STATEMENTS PERFORMED IN ACCORDANCE WITH GOVERNMENT AUDITING STANDARDS

The Federal Financial Institutions Examination Council:

We have audited the financial statements of the Federal Financial Institutions Examination Council (the "Council") as of and for the year ended December 31, 2009, and have issued our report thereon dated March 9, 2010. We conducted our audit in accordance with auditing standards generally accepted in the United States of America and the standards applicable to financial audits contained in *Government Auditing Standards*, issued by the Comptroller General of the United States.

Internal Control over Financial Reporting

In planning and performing our audit, we considered the Council's internal control over financial reporting as a basis for designing our auditing procedures for the purpose of expressing our opinion on the financial statements, but not for the purpose of expressing an opinion on the effectiveness of the Council's internal control over financial reporting. Accordingly, we do not express an opinion on the effectiveness of the Council's internal control over financial reporting.

A *control deficiency* exists when the design or operation of a control does not allow management or employees, in the normal course of performing their assigned functions, to prevent or detect misstatements on a timely basis. A significant deficiency is a control deficiency, or combination of control deficiencies, that adversely affects the entity's ability to initiate, authorize, record, process, or report financial data reliably in accordance with generally accepted accounting principles such that there is more than a remote likelihood that a misstatement of the Council's financial statements that is more than inconsequential will not be prevented or detected by the Council's internal control.

A *material weakness* is a significant deficiency, or combination of significant deficiencies, that results in more than a remote likelihood that a material misstatement of the financial statements will not be prevented or detected by the Council's internal control.

Our consideration of internal control over financial reporting was for the limited purpose described in the first paragraph of this section and would not necessarily identify all deficiencies in internal control that might be significant deficiencies or material weaknesses. We did not identify any deficiencies in internal control over financial reporting that we consider to be material weaknesses, as defined above.

Member of
Deloitte Touche Tohmatsu

Compliance and Other Matters

As part of obtaining reasonable assurance about whether the Council's financial statements are free of material misstatement, we performed tests of its compliance with certain provisions of laws, regulations, contracts, and grant agreements, noncompliance with which could have a direct and material effect on the determination of financial statement amounts. However, providing an opinion on compliance with those provisions was not an objective of our audit, and accordingly, we do not express such an opinion. The results of our tests disclosed no instances of noncompliance or other matters that are required to be reported under *Government Auditing Standards*.

Distribution

This report is intended solely for the information and use of the Council, management, and others within the organization, and the Office of Inspector General, and the United States Congress, and is not intended to be and should not be used by anyone other than these specified parties.

Deloitte + Touche LLP

McLean, VA
March 9, 2010

APPENDIX C: MAPS OF AGENCY REGIONS AND DISTRICTS

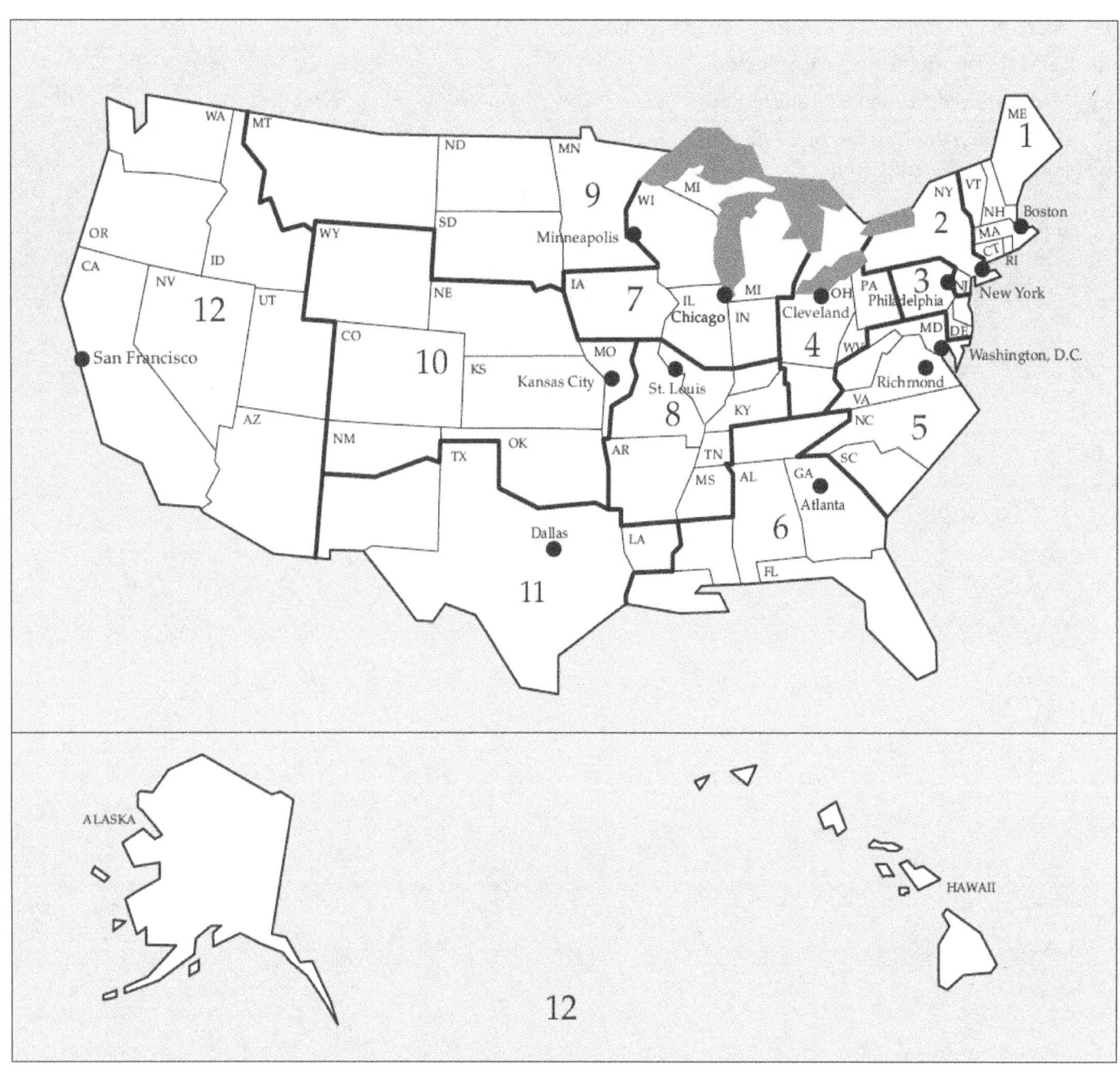

FEDERAL DEPOSIT INSURANCE CORPORATION REGIONS
(SUPERVISION AND COMPLIANCE)

* Two area offices are located in Boston
  (reports to New York) and Memphis
  (reports to Dallas)

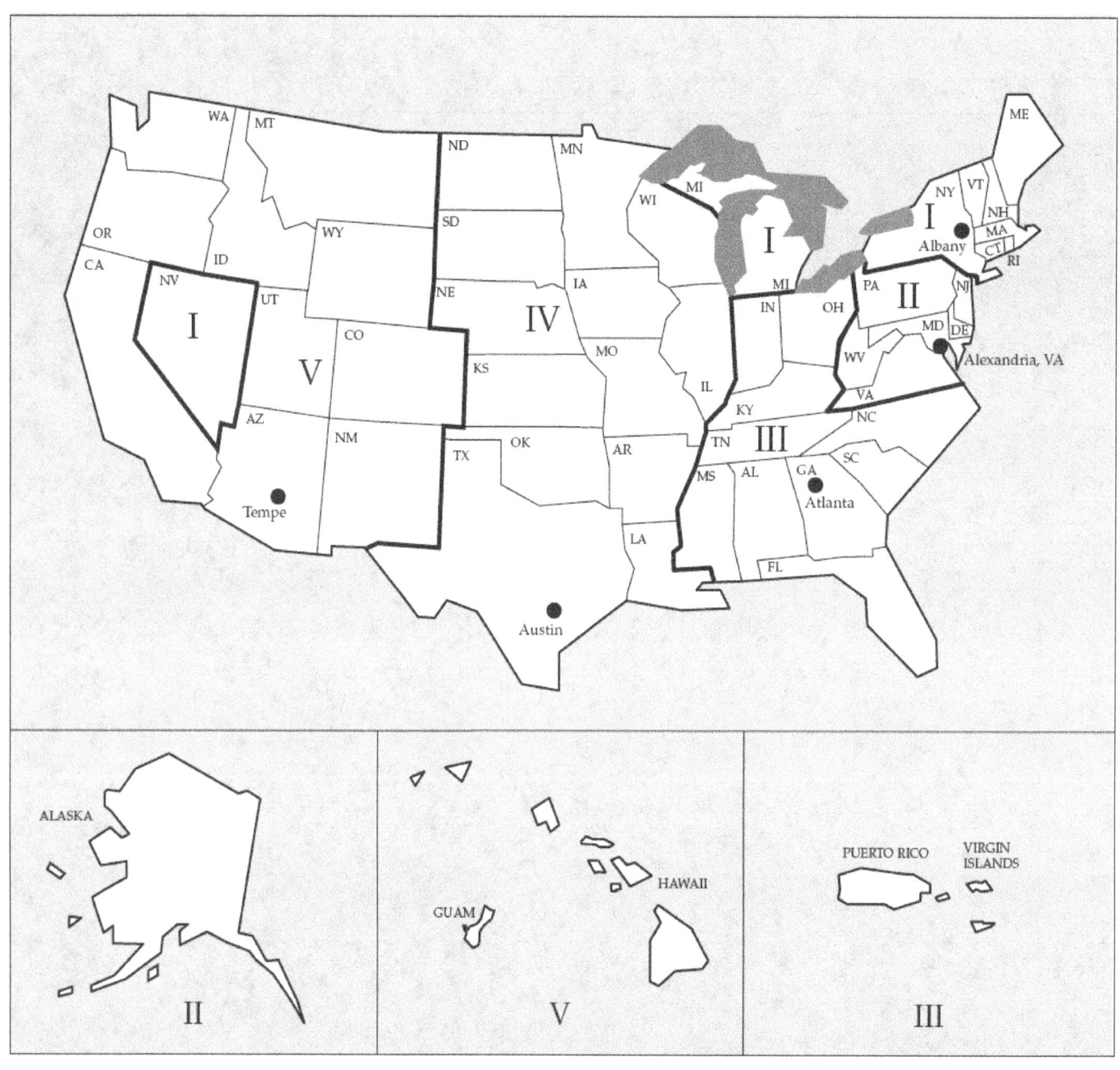

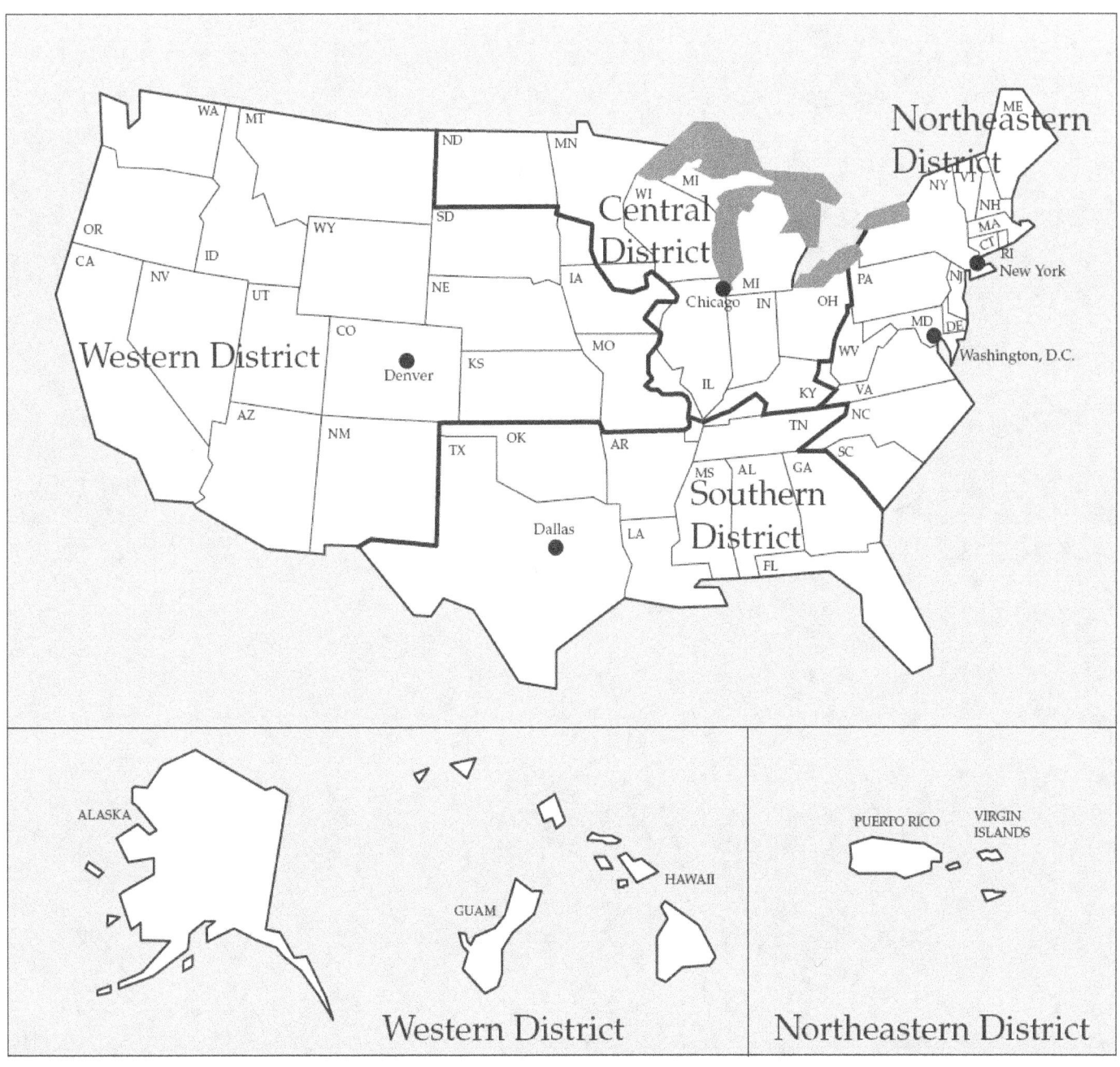

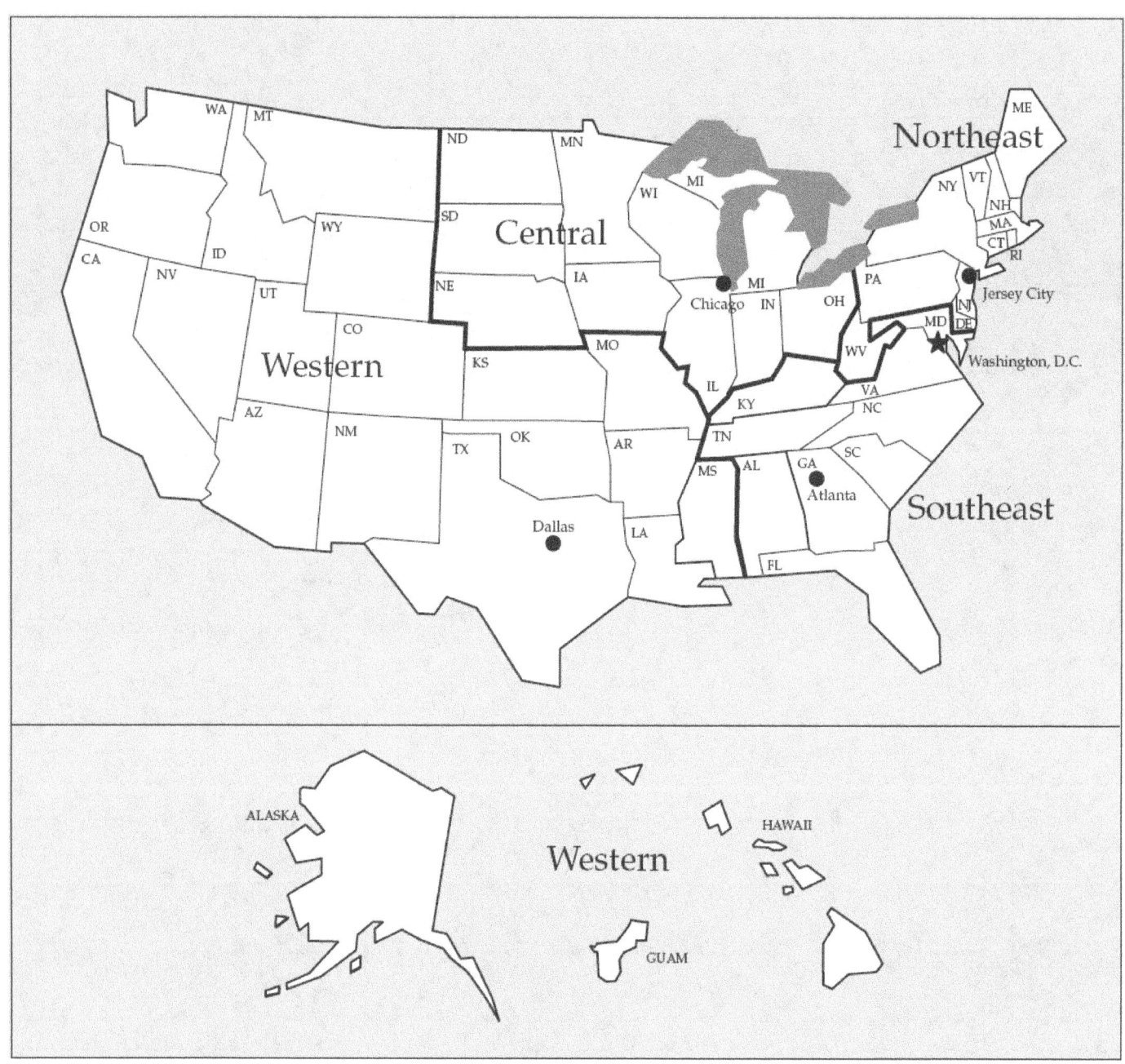

Organization, December 31, 2009

Members of the Council

Sheila C. Bair, *Chairman*
Chairperson
Federal Deposit Insurance
Corporation (FDIC)

John E. Bowman, *Vice Chairman*
Acting Director
Office of Thrift Supervision (OTS)

Debbie Matz
Chairman
National Credit Union
Administration (NCUA)

John C. Dugan
Comptroller of the Currency
Office of the Comptroller of the
Currency (OCC)

Daniel K. Tarullo
Member
Board of Governors of the Federal
Reserve System (FRB)

John Munn
State Liaison Committee (SLC)
Chairman
Director
Nebraska Department of Banking
& Finance

State Liaison Committee (SLC)

John Munn, *Chairman*
Director
Nebraska Department of Banking
& Finance

Harold E. Feeney
Commissioner
Texas Credit Union Department

Douglas Foster
Commissioner
Texas Department of Savings and
Mortgage Lending

Sarah Bloom Raskin
Commissioner
Maryland Office of the
Commissioner of Financial
Regulation

Charles A. Vice
Commissioner
Kentucky Department of
Financial Institutions

Council Staff Officer

Paul T. Sanford
Executive Secretary

Interagency Staff Groups

Agency Liaison Group

Sandra Thompson (FDIC)
Thomas A. Barnes (OTS)
Melinda Love (NCUA)
Tim Long (OCC)
Barbara Bouchard (FRB)
Michael Stevens (SLC Chair
Representative)

Legal Advisory Group

Michael Bradfield, *Chairman* (FDIC)
Deborah Dakin (OTS)
Robert M. Fenner (NCUA)
Julie L. Williams (OCC)
Scott Alvarez, (FRB)
Sarah Bloom Raskin (SLC Chair
Representative)

Task Force on Consumer Compliance

Luke H. Brown, *Chairman* (FDIC)
David Cotney (SLC Chair
Representative)
Ann Jaedicke (OCC)
Joy Lee (NCUA)
Glenn E. Loney (FRB)
Montrice G. Yakimov (OTS)

Task Force on Examiner Education

Cheryl Davis, *Chairman* (OCC)
Dana E. Payne, *Vice Chairman* (FRB)
Charlotte Buchanan (SLC Chair
Representative)
Ronald Dice (OTS)
Joy Lee (NCUA)
Betty J. Rudolph (FDIC)

Task Force on Information Sharing

Michael Kraemer, *Chairman* (FRB)
Dave Godwin (OTS)
John Kolhoff (SLC Chair
Representative)
Dominick Nigro (NCUA)
Jaime J. Perez (FDIC)
Robin Stefan (OCC)

Task Force on Reports

Robert F. Storch, *Chairman* (FDIC)
James Caton (OTS)
Dale Jacobs (SLC Chair
Representative)
Arthur Lindo (FRB)
Kathy K. Murphy (OCC)
R. Ashley Rowe (NCUA)

Task Force on Supervision

Thomas A. Barnes, *Chairman* (OTS)
Patrick M. Parkinson (FRB)
Joy Lee (NCUA)
Tim Long (OCC)
Sandra Thompson (FDIC)
Charles A. Vice (SLC Chair
Representative)

Task Force on Surveillance Systems

Robin Stefan, *Chairman* (OCC)
Bob Bacon (SLC Chair
Representative)
James Caton (OTS)
Charles Collier (FDIC)
Matt Mattson (FRB)
R. Ashley Rowe (NCUA)

Staff Members of the FFIEC

Shown are the FFIEC staff members at the Seidman Center in Arlington, Virginia, where they have their offices and classrooms for examiner education programs.

Federal Financial Institutions Examination Council staff members (from the left to right): John Smullen, Ernest Larkins, Catherine Pritchard, Darlene Callis, Paul Sanford, Michelle Clark, Jennifer Herring, Karen Smith, Cynthia Curry-Daniel, Rosanna Piccirilli, and Juliet Pradier.

1979

Council Chairman: John G. Heimann, Comptroller of the Currency, Office of Comptroller of the Currency (OCC)

Council Vice Chairman: Lawrence Connell, Jr., Chairman, National Credit Union Administration (NCUA)

Council Members: Jay Janis, Chairman, Federal Home Loan Bank Board (FHLBB); J. Charles Partee, Member, Board of Governors of the Federal Reserve System (FRB); and Irvine H. Sprague, Chairman, Federal Deposit Insurance Corporation (FDIC)

State Liaison Committee (SLC) Chairman: William L. Cole, Administrator, Office of Savings & Loans, North Carolina

Council Executive Secretary: Robert J. Lawrence

1980

Council Chairman: John G. Heimann, Comptroller of the Currency, OCC

Council Vice Chairman: Lawrence Connell, Jr., Chairman, NCUA

Council Members: John H. Dalton, Chairman, FHLBB; J. Charles Partee, Member, FRB; and Irvine H. Sprague, Chairman FDIC

SLC Chairman: Muriel F. Siebert, Superintendant of Banks, New York

Council Executive Secretary: Robert J. Lawrence

1981

Council Chairman: J. Charles Partee, Member, FRB

Council Vice Chairman: William M. Isaac, Chairman, FDIC

Council Members: Edgar F. Callahan, Chairman, NCUA; C. T. Conover, Comptroller of the Currency, OCC; and Richard T. Pratt, Chairman, FHLBB

SLC Chairman: William C. Harris, Commissioner, Division of Banks and Trust Companies, Illinois

Council Executive Secretary: Robert J. Lawrence

1982

Council Chairman: J. Charles Partee, Member, FRB

Council Vice Chairman: William M. Isaac, Chairman, FDIC

Council Members: Edgar F. Callahan, Chairman, NCUA; C. T. Conover, Comptroller of the Currency, OCC; and Richard T. Pratt, Chairman, FHLBB

SLC Chairman: Edward D. Dunn, Commissioner, Department of Banking and Finance, Georgia

Council Executive Secretary: Robert J. Lawrence

1983　*Council Chairman:* William M. Isaac, Chairman, FDIC

　　　Council Vice Chairman: Edwin J. Gray, Chairman, FHLBB

　　　Council Members: Edgar F. Callahan, Chairman, NCUA; C. T. Conover, Comptroller of the Currency, OCC; and J. Charles Partee, Member, FRB

　　　SLC Chairman: William C. Harris, Commissioner, Division of Banks and Trust Companies, Illinois

　　　Council Executive Secretary: Robert J. Lawrence

1984　*Council Chairman:* William M. Isaac, Chairman, FDIC

　　　Council Vice Chairman: Edwin J. Gray, Chairman, FHLBB

　　　Council Members: Edgar F. Callahan, Chairman, NCUA; C. T. Conover, Comptroller of the Currency, OCC; and J. Charles Partee, Member, FRB

　　　SLC Chairman: Sidney A. Bailey, Commissioner of Financial Institutions, Virginia

　　　Council Executive Secretary: Robert J. Lawrence

1985　*Council Chairman:* Edwin J. Gray, Chairman, FHLBB

　　　Council Vice Chairman: Robert L. Clarke, Comptroller of the Currency, OCC

　　　Council Members: Roger W. Jepsen, Chairman, NCUA; J. Charles Partee, Member, FRB; and L. William Seidman, Chairman, FDIC

　　　SLC Chairman: Sidney A. Bailey, Commissioner of Financial Institutions, Virginia

　　　Council Executive Secretary: Robert J. Lawrence

1986　*Council Chairman:* Edwin J. Gray, Chairman, FHLBB

　　　Council Vice Chairman: Robert L. Clarke, Comptroller of the Currency, OCC

　　　Council Members: Roger W. Jepsen, Chairman, NCUA; Manuel H. Johnson, Vice Chairman, FRB; and L. William Seidman, Chairman, FDIC

　　　SLC Chairman: Sidney A. Bailey, Commissioner of Financial Institutions, Virginia

　　　Council Executive Secretary: Robert J. Lawrence

1987　*Council Chairman:* Roger W. Jepsen, Chairman, NCUA

　　　Council Vice Chairman: Robert L. Clarke, Comptroller of the Currency, OCC

　　　Council Members: H. Robert Heller, Member, FRB; L. William Seidman, Chairman, FDIC; and M. Danny Wall, Chairman, FHLBB

　　　SLC Chairman: Michael N. Fitzgerald, Director, Credit Union Division, Michigan

　　　Council Executive Secretary: Robert J. Lawrence

1988　*Council Chairman:* Roger W. Jepsen, Chairman, NCUA

　　　　Council Vice Chairman: Robert L. Clarke, Comptroller of the Currency, OCC

　　　　Council Members: H. Robert Heller, Member, FRB; L. William Seidman, Chairman, FDIC; and M. Danny Wall, Chairman, FHLBB

　　　　SLC Chairman: Mary C. Short, Superintendent of Banks, Arizona

　　　　Council Executive Secretary: Robert J. Lawrence

1989　*Council Chairman:* Robert L. Clarke, Comptroller of the Currency, OCC

　　　　Council Vice Chairman: John P. LaWare, Member, FRB

　　　　Council Members: Roger W. Japsen, Chairman, NCUA; L. William Seidman, Chairman, FDIC; and M. Danny Wall, Chairman, Office of Thrift Supervision (OTS)

　　　　SLC Chairman: John R. Hale, Credit Union Commissioner, Texas

　　　　Council Executive Secretary: Robert J. Lawrence

1990　*Council Chairman:* Robert L. Clarke, Comptroller of the Currency, OCC

　　　　Council Vice Chairman: John P. LaWare, Member, FRB

　　　　Council Members: Roger W. Japsen, Chairman, NCUA; T. Timothy Ryan, Director, OTS and L. William Seidman, Chairman, FDIC

　　　　SLC Chairman: John R. Hale, Credit Union Commissioner, Texas

　　　　Council Executive Secretary: Robert J. Lawrence

1991　*Council Chairman:* John P. LaWare, Member, FRB

　　　　Council Vice Chairman: William Taylor, Chairman, FDIC

　　　　Council Members: Robert L. Clarke, Comptroller of the Currency, OCC; Roger W. Japsen, Chairman, NCUA; and T. Timothy Ryan, Director, OTS

　　　　SLC Chairman: James E. Gilleran, Superintendent of Banks, California

　　　　Council Executive Secretary: Joe M. Cleaver

1992　*Council Chairman:* John P. LaWare, Member, FRB

　　　　Council Vice Chairman: Andrew C. Hove, Jr., Acting Chairman, FDIC

　　　　Council Members: Jonathan L. Fiechter, Acting Director, OTS; Roger W. Japsen, Chairman, NCUA; and Stephen R. Steinbrink, Acting Comptroller of the Currency, OCC

　　　　SLC Chairman: James E. Gilleran, Superintendent of Banks, California

　　　　Council Executive Secretary: Joe M. Cleaver

1993

Council Chairman: Andrew C. Hove, Jr., Acting Chairman, FDIC

Council Vice Chairman: Jonathan L. Fiechter, Acting Director, OTS

Council Members: Norman E. D'Amours, Chairman, NCUA; John P. LaWare, Member, FRB; and Eugene A. Ludwig, Comptroller of the Currency, OCC

SLC Chairman: Margie H. Muller, State Bank Commissioner, Maryland

Council Executive Secretary: Joe M. Cleaver

1994

Council Chairman: Ricki Tigert Helfer, Chairman, FDIC

Council Vice Chairman: Jonathan L. Fiechter, Acting Director, OTS

Council Members: Norman E. D'Amours, Chairman, NCUA; John P. LaWare, Member, FRB; and Eugene A. Ludwig, Comptroller of the Currency, OCC

SLC Chairman: Harold N. Lee, Jr., Commissioner, Office of Commissioner of Savings and Loan, Wisconsin

Council Executive Secretary: Joe M. Cleaver

1995

Council Chairman: Jonathan L. Fiechter, Acting Director, OTS

Council Vice Chairman: Norman E. D'Amours, Chairman, NCUA

Council Members: Ricki Tigert Helfer, Chairman, FDIC; Edward W. Kelley, Jr., Member, FRB; and Eugene A. Ludwig, Comptroller of the Currency, OCC

SLC Chairman: Harold N. Lee, Jr., Commissioner, Office of Commissioner of Savings and Loan, Wisconsin

Council Executive Secretary: Joe M. Cleaver

1996

Council Chairman: Nicolas P. Retsinas, Director, OTS

Council Vice Chairman: Norman E. D'Amours, Chairman, NCUA

Council Members: Ricki Tigert Helfer, Chairman, FDIC; Eugene A. Ludwig, Comptroller of the Currency, OCC; and Susan M. Phillips, Member, FRB

SLC Chairman: Gavin M. Gee, Jr., Director, Department of Finance, Idaho

Council Executive Secretary: Joe M. Cleaver

1997

Council Chairman: Eugene A. Ludwig, Comptroller of the Currency, OCC

Council Vice Chairman: Susan M. Phillips, Member, FRB

Council Members: Norman E. D'Amours, Chairman, NCUA; Andrew C. Hove, Acting Chairman, FDIC; and Ellen Seidman, Director, OTS

SLC Chairman: Gavin M. Gee, Jr., Director, Department of Finance, Idaho

Council Executive Secretary: Joe M. Cleaver

1998   *Council Chairman:* John D. Hawke, Jr., Comptroller of the Currency, OCC

       Council Vice Chairman: Lawrence H. Meyer, Member, FRB

       Council Members: Norman E. D'Amours, Chairman, NCUA; Donna Tanoue, Chairman, FDIC; and Ellen Seidman, Director, OTS

       SLC Chairman: Thomas J. Curry, Commissioner of Banks, Massachusetts

       Council Executive Secretary: Keith J. Todd

1999   *Council Chairman:* Lawrence H. Meyer, Member, FRB

       Council Vice Chairman: Donna Tanoue, Chairman, FDIC

       Council Members: Norman E. D'Amours, Chairman, NCUA; John D. Hawke, Jr., Comptroller of the Currency, OCC; and Ellen Seidman, Director, OTS

       SLC Chairman: G. Edward Leary, Commissioner of Financial Institutions, Utah

       Council Executive Secretary: Keith J. Todd

2000   *Council Chairman:* Lawrence H. Meyer, Member, FRB

       Council Vice Chairman: Donna Tanoue, Chairman, FDIC

       Council Members: Norman E. D'Amours, Chairman, NCUA; John D. Hawke, Jr., Comptroller of the Currency, OCC; and Ellen Seidman, Director, OTS

       SLC Chairman: G. Edward Leary, Commissioner of Financial Institutions, Utah

       Council Executive Secretary: Keith J. Todd

2001   *Council Chairman:* Donald E. Powell, Chairman, FDIC

       Council Vice Chairman: James E. Gilleran, Director, OTS

       Council Members: Dennis Dollar, Chairman, NCUA; John D. Hawke, Jr., Comptroller of the Currency, OCC; and Lawrence H. Meyer, Member, FRB

       SLC Chairman: G. Edward Leary, Commissioner of Financial Institutions, Utah

       Council Executive Secretary: Keith J. Todd

2002   *Council Chairman:* Donald E. Powell, Chairman, FDIC

       Council Vice Chairman: James E. Gilleran, Director, OTS

       Council Members: Susan Schmidt Bies, Member, FRB; Dennis Dollar, Chairman, NCUA; and John D. Hawke, Jr., Comptroller of the Currency, OCC

       SLC Chairman: John S. Allison, Commissioner, Department of Banking and Consumer Finance

       Council Executive Secretary: Vacant

2003   *Council Chairman:* James E. Gilleran, Director, OTS

Council Vice Chairman: Dennis Dollar, Chairman, NCUA

Council Members: Susan Schmidt Bies, Member, FRB; John D. Hawke, Jr., Comptroller of the Currency, OCC; and Donald E. Powell, Chairman, FDIC

SLC Chairman: John S. Allison, Commissioner, Department of Banking and Consumer Finance

Council Executive Secretary: Tamara J. Wiseman

2004   *Council Chairman:* James E. Gilleran, Director, OTS

Council Vice Chairman: JoAnn Johnson, Chairman, NCUA

Council Members: Susan Schmidt Bies, Member, FRB; Donald E. Powell, Chairman, FDIC; and Julie L. Williams, Acting Comptroller of the Currency, OCC

SLC Chairman: Richard C. Houseworth, Superintendant of Banks, Arizona

Council Executive Secretary: Tamara J. Wiseman

2005   *Council Chairman:* John C. Dugan, Comptroller of the Currency, OCC

Council Vice Chairman: Susan Schmidt Bies, Member, FRB

Council Members: Martin J. Guenberg, Acting Chairman, FDIC; JoAnn Johnson, Chairman, NCUA; and John M. Reich, Director, OTS

SLC Chairman: Richard C. Houseworth, Superintendant of Banks, Arizona

Council Executive Secretary: Tamara J. Wiseman

2006   *Council Chairman:* John C. Dugan, Comptroller of the Currency, OCC

Council Vice Chairman: Susan Schmidt Bies, Member, FRB

Council Members: Steven L. Antonakes, SLC Chairman, Commissioner of Banks, MA; Sheila C. Bair, Chairman, FDIC; JoAnn Johnson, Chairman, NCUA; and John M. Reich, Director, OTS

Council Executive Secretary: Tamara J. Wiseman

2007   *Council Chairman:* Randall Kroszner, Member, FRB

Council Vice Chairman: Sheila C. Bair, Chairman, FDIC

Council Members: Steven L. Antonakes, SLC Chairman, Commissioner of Banks, MA; John C. Dugan, Comptroller of the Currency, OCC; JoAnn Johnson, Chairman, NCUA; and John M. Reich, Director, OTS

Council Executive Secretary: Tamara J. Wiseman

2008   *Council Chairman:* Randall Kroszner, Member, FRB

Council Vice Chairman: Sheila C. Bair, Chairman, FDIC

Council Members: John C. Dugan, Comptroller of the Currency, OCC; Michael E. Fryzel, Chairman, NCUA; John Munn, SLC Chairman, Director, Department of Banking & Finance, NE; and John M. Reich, Director, OTS

Council Executive Secretary: Paul T. Sanford

2009   *Council Chairman:* Sheila C. Bair, Chairman, FDIC

Council Vice Chairman: John E. Bowman, Acting Director, OTS

Council Members: Debbie Matz, Chairman, NCUA; John C. Dugan, Comptroller of the Currency, OCC; John Munn, SLC Chairman, Director, Department of Banking & Finance, NE; Daniel K. Tarullo, Member, FRB

Council Executive Secretary: Paul T. Sanford